Beyond Monotheism

Beyond Monotheism

Discerning the Sacredness in Nature

DONALD A. CROSBY

Published by State University of New York Press, Albany

EU GPSR Authorised Representative:
Logos Europe, 9 rue Nicolas Poussin, 17000, La Rochelle, France
contact@logoseurope.eu

For information, contact State University of New York Press, Albany, NY
www.sunypress.edu

Library of Congress Cataloging-in-Publication Data

Name: Crosby, Donald A. author
Title: Beyond monotheism : discerning the sacredness in nature / Donald A. Crosby.
Description: Albany : State University of New York Press, [2025] | Series: SUNY series on religion and the environment | Includes bibliographical references and index.
Identifiers: LCCN 2025012565 | ISBN 9798855804140 (hardcover : alk. paper | ISBN 9798855804164 (ebook) | ISBN 9798855804157 (pbk. : alk. paper)
Subjects: LCSH: Nature—Religious aspects | Naturalism—Religious aspects | Monotheism
Classification: LCC BL65.N35 C755 2025 | DDC 202/.12—dc23/eng/20250324
LC record available at https://lccn.loc.gov/2025012565

Contents

Acknowledgments

I thank James Peltz, editor-in-chief of SUNY Press and Diane Ganeles, senior production editor, for their patience and care in working with me on this book through its stages of consideration and development. I am also deeply indebted to my wife, Pam, for reading and commenting on the manuscript throughout its process of being written. Finally, I gratefully acknowledge the comments, suggestions, and critical questions raised about an earlier draft by two perceptive anonymous readers assigned to this task by SUNY.

Introduction

The great majority of those presently committed to a religion that centers on a monotheistic God, at least presently in the West, tend to take for granted the conviction that religion as such and belief in one God are synonymous. *Atheism, secularism,* and *non-religion* are deemed to be different terms for the same outlook and way of life. Religion is thus assumed to have no meaning apart from belief in God. But what is the basis for such an assumption? The three great religious traditions that originated in the Middle East and have also become dominant in the West, namely, Judaism, Christianity, and Islam, have contended since their inceptions that their basis is not in unaided human experience or reason but in divine initiative and the binding authority of divine revelation.

God reaches down to humans and makes Godself known, disclosing to humans not only God's loving presence, but the point and purpose, the duties and obligations, the fundamental and saving significance of their lives on earth. They are taught by God through God's chosen human spokespersons that they are creatures of God and should be bound to God in heart, mind, and will. The existence of a personal God is not questioned in this perspective because God is believed to have taken the initiative, and God's revelatory initiative is held to lie at the core of authentic religious faith. Reason, experience, and practice grow out of and give expression to this initiative. But they do not—*and cannot*—substitute for it or attain *by themselves* its crucial truths for thought, commitment, and life.

Not even the splendor and fullness of divine revelation itself can begin to exhaust the gracious and unutterable meaning of God's saving presence, power, and glory. To try to arrive at the existence and nature of God by human reason alone would be a futile endeavor in this way of thinking. To use a simile I have used elsewhere, it would be like trying, unaided, to climb to the top of a huge vertical panel of glass, hoping finally to discover and comprehend the reality of God who resides there. Such an imagined task would afford us no purchase, no means of ascent within human ingenuity or control. If there is a God, that awesome, unattainable God would have to reach down to us from the top of the lofty panel and lift us up.

Otherwise, nothing of dependable belief or saving significance could be known about God. Abraham at the cutting of the covenant; Moses at the burning bush; Isaiah in the temple; the response of the fishermen to Jesus's call and to his person, teaching, and mission; Paul on the road to Damascus; Muhammad in the cave at Mecca being commanded by Allah's angelic emissary to recite each of the passages of what would become the Holy Qur'an: all of these and many other such momentous events and experiences are examples of claimed revelation. Their accounts in the sacred scriptures of Judaism, Christianity, and Islam are regarded as the ultimate bases of theistic faith in these three religious traditions.

The bases have been carried forward to the present by revered teachers who seek to explicate their meanings but who do not purport to arrive at them by human reason or human experience alone. Reason and experience are brought into explicative and applicative play, of course, but they are subordinated to the absolute inspiration and authority of revelation. The existence of God is *assumed* in such investigative practices, not, in the final analysis, thought to be capable of being argued for, reasoned, or proved. Reason and experience are the humble servants of divine revelation, not its ultimate sources or masters. Moreover, the God made known by revelation is held by traditional theists to be a distinct, living *Person*, not merely a concept, ideal, or abstraction—a Person whose nature, will, and purpose are made known by the loving initiative of that divine Person's encounters with human persons on earth, persons assumed to be creatures of this eminently personal God.

In the first chapter, I focus on two relatively recent such teachers or explicators of the meanings of divine revelation: the Protestant Christian Søren Kierkegaard in the nineteenth century CE and the Jewish theologian Martin Buber in the twentieth. Other examples could of course be used as well, but these can serve as examples of a monotheistic version of religion grounded in putative revelations believed to be by and about the one true God. Kierkegaard, in particular, lays heavy emphasis on the paradoxicality of divine revelation, insisting that such paradoxicality is only what should be expected in revelations that stem from a mysterious and radically transcendent God.

I also want us to consider some objections to this idea: a task I take up in this chapter and to a fuller extent in chapter 2 with consideration of some of the criticisms of revelatory monotheism brought forcibly into view by the nineteenth-century German philosopher Ludwig Feuerbach. The thesis I shall defend in this second chapter is that an alleged absolute authority of divine revelation cannot be set in sharp, dualistic contrast with human experience and reason. Its authority would be of little use or even comprehension were it not filtered through fallible, debatable human interpretations in every age. The hand of the human lies heavily over all purported divine revelations—in both their initial receptions and also in their subsequent interpretations. Feuerbach's discussion helps to make this idea abundantly clear.

It is therefore extremely important to subject alleged divine revelations regularly to the courts of human experience and reason but always to do so in a respectful, open-minded spirit. An uninterpreted revelation is a useless revelation. We cannot meaningfully set mere *recitation* in the place of *interpretation*—a static set of fixed beliefs cannot replace the ongoing task of striving to make sense of alleged revelation in the contexts of changing circumstances and changing times. A claim to revelation must be continually verified in ongoing life and thought; it cannot just be assumed. Such a view is not arrogant but necessary. And it must be brought to the test of every generation and by each of those who lay claim to its truth if it is to continue to have its purported meaning and value. An alleged, merely taken for granted, unquestioned, and untested revelation will have no revelatory power. How it is to be tested is an issue we shall continue to raise in this book.

In Feuerbach's view, as we shall see in chapter 2, the initiators of so-called revelations are human beings, not God, and the imagined personal God is a projection of human sensitivity and reason, along with human longing and hope. For him, it is not so much that we are created in the image of God as that God is created in the image of humans.

Chapter 3 offers an explication and interpretation of the theology of the German philosophical theologian Paul Tillich, who spent much of his career teaching and writing in the United States after leaving Germany during the early years of the establishment of the Nazi state. We will see that he takes a different tack than Kierkegaard and Buber, on the one hand, and Feuerbach, on the other, assuming the idea of divine disclosure in his own thoughtful manner but casting it in a different, more purely philosophical but also highly symbolical mold.

Tillich's theology was deeply attuned to and influenced by the cultural currents of his tumultuous time, which encompassed two devastatingly destructive world wars. He was especially sensitive to its Freudian and Jungian depth psychology (or psychology that pays special attention to the role of the human unconsciousness) and existentialist philosophy, the latter primarily that of his fellow German, Martin Heidegger. Tillich also placed strong emphasis on the inability of literal language to do justice to religious truth, an emphasis with special bearing on his conception of God. He was particularly critical of the idea that God exists as a distinctive personal being among other existent beings and argued that God must be recognized as Being-Itself or the Ground of all existent beings, including human beings.

Chapter 4 examines the philosophical basis laid out by the German thinker Friedrich Wilhelm Joseph von Schelling for conviction of the existence of God as creator of the world, and then supplementing this rational analysis with interpretations of the nature and purpose of the Triune God of Christian revelation. Schelling's nineteenth-century rational or a priori approach to the existence of God anticipates in an important manner Tillich's key conception of God as Being-Itself in the twentieth century, as I show in this chapter, and his explication of some major themes in purported Christian revelation is intriguing and insightful.

Tillich wrote two dissertations on Schelling's philosophy for his licentiate and doctor of philosophy degrees, respectively, and he was notably fond of Schelling's philosophy of nature. I discuss Schelling's nineteenth-century philosophy in its relation to Christian revelation *after* Tillich's similar enterprise in the twentieth century for *thematic* rather than *chronological* reasons. In doing so, I want to do at least some justice to Schelling's influence on Tillich's thought in order to add to my explication of particular features of the latter's better-known and highly influential twentieth-century thought that was brought into view in the previous chapter.

Since much of my religion of nature, the defense of which I develop in chapters 7 and 8, takes seriously developments of recent natural science, I critically assess in chapter five the arguments of English physicist-theologian John Polkinghorne to the effect that contemporary physics points the way reliably and assuredly to the reality of a personal God. Physics can certainly help to exhibit the compatibility of natural science with a religion of nature, but I do not agree with Polkinghorne that it provides definitive evidence for the existence of a personal deity, and I explain why I do not.

Chapter 6 presents and evaluates some major lines of argument for the character and existence of the traditional Christian conception of God that are set forth and developed by another English philosophical theologian, Richard Swinburne. I take issue with much of his reasoning in this regard and explain why I do not find it convincing. His work is especially valuable in my judgment, however, because the views he defends are largely traditional. Moreover, he endeavors to support these views with considerable firsthand reflection and carefully developed arguments that call for critical assessment.

My references to the claims, arguments, and insights of these seven thinkers prepare the way for my own analysis in chapter 7 of the continuing meaning and importance of religious faith, one that will focus not on a personal and yet somehow radically transcendent God but on the pervasive immanence of sacred meaning, value, and importance in nature itself. A religion of nature is well worth consideration as a possibly more adequate, readily available, and currently more intelligible, convincing way—at least in my judgment—of approaching and understanding the needs, hopes, and aspirations of religious faith in our own time.

I do not for a moment propose that we substitute *secular* culture, with its own distinctive forms of secular faith,[1] for *religion* or for meaningful *religious* faith. Living religious faith stands in need of constant concourse with secular culture—as Paul Tillich constantly and persuasively maintained—but it cannot be reduced to or subsumed under secular culture. I do propose, however, that alongside a traditional religious faith, centered on a radically transcendent and yet fundamentally personal God, we should place a profound sensitivity next to the inexhaustibly inspiring, saving, and demanding sacredness of the surrounding nature that includes us human creatures along with all of the other forms of natural life on earth. This approach to religious faith can incorporate and carry forward many of the motifs of theistic religion, but without ultimate reliance on the assumed existence, role, or revelatory manifestation of the will and purposes of a personal God.

Therefore, following my critical discussions of the interpretations of theism provided by Kierkegaard, Buber, Feuerbach, Tillich, Schelling, Polkinghorne, and Swinburne, chapter 7 develops some central features of religious naturalism or of *A Religion of Nature*, as I have come over the years to interpret, understand, elaborate, and defend it.

Then in chapter 8, I supplement my defense of a nontheistic religious naturalism with a defense of it by three other esteemed thinkers, one a physics professor, Chet Raymo; another, a theoretical biologist, Stuart A. Kauffman; and the third, a philosopher, Carol Wayne White. In citing the first two, I take further issue with Polkinghorne's contention that the natural sciences—and especially his discipline of physics—give formidable support, when properly interpreted and understood, to a monotheistic metaphysical outlook and type of religious faith.

It is important for my readers to understand that it is not merely for argument's sake that I register my strong disagreements with monotheists, especially monotheists of the extremely high intellectual, moral, and religious character such as those I discuss in this book. I do not wish to cross swords with them; I only refer to them as a way of explicating the theistic points of view I have come to disagree with over the years and to explain the grounds of my disagreement with them as ways of contextualizing and presenting my own current form of religious faith.

I view these monotheistic thinkers not as adversaries but as dialogue partners in a common enterprise, and I hope that my expositions and criticisms of their thought will be reflected on by my readers in a dialogical, not an adversarial, manner. I devote this book to an explication and defense of religious naturalism because I think that it holds considerable promise as a way of thinking religiously and developing a relevant, sustaining, and meaningful religious faith in today's world. Scientific understandings of nature are increasingly common to us all in our increasingly global civilization in a way that a monotheistic Jewish, Christian, or Islamic God is not. But nature here on earth is also being increasingly endangered by our calloused attitudes and actions toward it in an increasingly technological, fossil-fuel-based civilization.

In the final analysis, I do not so much reject traditional monotheism's conception of God as I find it, with all of its familiar paradoxes and perplexities, as unnecessary baggage in the pursuit of religious truth and commitment to these truths. Properly regarded and responded to religiously, the sacredness of nature, the gifts it bestows on us, and the responsibilities with which it endows us as human beings are so wondrous, grave, purposeful, and demanding as to leave little room or need for pondering the perplexities of traditional belief in God. Nature, in my humble judgment, is an entirely sufficient focus of religious commitment and dedication of life.

Our home is here, and our religious and moral aspirations and responsibilities should be focused here, not on some imagined or dreamed-of other realm of being. We do not need to *escape* nature religiously. We need to *explore* and *engage* it religiously and with much more purpose and responsibility than we have in the past. It is incumbent on us to acknowledge with full awareness that being natural is the common character of all of us, human and nonhuman alike, on this earth and elsewhere in the cosmos—if, as is entirely likely, there are other life forms elsewhere in the vast cosmos than just on our little planet. We humans on earth are natural beings through and through, and our moral and religious privileges, opportunities, and obligations are natural. We have no crying need for anything supernatural.

This is my credo as a convinced proponent of a religion of nature. Others may not see things in the same manner, but whoever thought that there could or would be universal consensus on profound religious questions? There has not been any such thing in the past, not even *within* particular historical religious communities, and it is very unlikely that there will be such in the future. What is entirely satisfying, supportive, and saving for one person may not prove such for another. And what is true in this respect for individual persons is also true for whole communities and whole civilizations, as human history makes abundantly clear.

Historically, religion has proved to be a many-splendored thing, not a monolithic thing. Attempts to make it the latter have proved to be destructive and abortive, and this continues to be an unassailable truth of our own time (for discussion of this point, see Crosby 2018b). Religion in its many different forms, including its multiple Indigenous ones, is a continuing source of inspiration and strength for diverse times and for different individuals and communities. Its diversity is its glory, not its blight.

In making this observation, I do not intend to endorse a relativistic conception of religious truth, but only to call attention to the elusiveness and ever-beckoning character of the age-long search for such truth. There is ample room for many different contestants in this enterprise, and it is essential that they continue to listen to and intently learn from one another. I have written this book with this conviction and in this spirit.

But in the meantime, we should not for a moment lose sight of the fact that what is common to all humans and to all other known forms of life is *nature*, not faith in a monotheistic *God*. The former is a unifying fact that underlies all of our differences and that demands our urgent attention in today's world. To neglect forceful and effective attention to the well-being of nature is to bring needless grave dangers to ourselves and to other life forms on earth. This is a ground of worldwide consensus that we should insist on recognizing and placing the strongest possible emphasis as underlying and informing all of our religious differences.

By way of concluding this introduction, I want to explain again my organization of this book. It is clearly not entirely chronological. I introduce Feuerbach in the nineteenth century, for example, after Buber in the twentieth, and I introduce Tillich in the twentieth century before his highly influential predecessor, Schelling, in the nineteenth century. I do so in these cases for thematic reasons, as previously explained, rather than chronological ones. While Kierkegaard and Buber are familiar representatives of a kind of monotheistic religion rooted in alleged divine revelations, Feuerbach is a perhaps less familiar critic today of Christian monotheism in particular and of its claimed basis in authoritative divine revelations. But his criticisms are astute, far-reaching, and worthy of continuing consideration, at least in my judgment.

Tillich's critique of a literalistic personal God in favor of seeing it as a symbolic representation of an existentially conceived, impersonal ground of being is more familiar, but the profound influences on his thought of the less familiar Schelling, whose reasoning substantially and lastingly influenced Tillich's later contributions to Christian philosophical theology, are less widely well known. So once again, my organization for my own critical discussion of these important nineteenth- and twentieth-century figures is not chronological but logical, part of an ongoing succession of interrelated arguments and counterarguments. Their dates are less important in this book than the interconnections of their modes of reasoning, whether positive or negative, that I want to bring into view. I could of course have chosen scores of other thinkers for similar purposes, but for better or worse, these five seem to me to be admirably suited to my purpose.

Chapter One

Revelatory Theism

Søren Kierkegaard

The Danish theologian, philosopher, and poet Søren Kierkegaard was a man of exceptional sensitivity and extraordinary—even if in many ways, quirky and unique—creative ability. He was also an unwaveringly serious and deeply committed Christian thinker throughout his life. His faith in the foundational importance of divine revelation was implicit in his every thought and action. I want to show this to be the case in his book, *Philosophical Fragments*. The modest title is characteristic of Kierkegaard's assumed role as a humble interpreter of the meaning of divine revelation and a subtle reminder that what is in question for him is not the absolute authority of the revelation itself, which he never presumes to doubt.

This work is admittedly *fragmentary* for its author because it turns on paradoxes of religious faith that cannot, in their very nature, be transformed into consistent, complete, unambiguous statements. Its issues cannot be untangled and resolved by even the most brilliant systematic efforts of abstract human speculation. These issues must be met, in the final analysis, by the stance of faith in its humble, receptive response to divine revelation, a revelation rooted in unresolvable paradox and irreducible conceptual inconsistency.

Kierkegaard writes that "if God does not exist it would of course be impossible to prove it, and if he does exist it would be folly to attempt it. . . . if when I speak of proving God's existence I mean to propose to prove that the Unknown, which exists, is God . . . I do not prove anything, least of all an existence, but merely develop the contents of a conception" (1952, 31). In other words, God and God's revelations to humankind that reach their consummate expression for Kierkegaard in the incarnation of God in Jesus of Nazareth, the God-Man, are not outcomes of speculative thought but of actions by the living God in human history.

Since the revelations are given to humans by God, Kierkegaard never questions the existence of God. He is a convinced monotheist from start to finish in his richly suggestive, highly influential, and brilliantly executed writing career. The keystone of his monotheism is his response to the New Testament accounts and interpretations of the life and teachings—nay, the sheer historical existence—of Jesus of Nazareth, whom Christian revelation regards as the incarnation of the one true God.

This existence is for him the pinnacle of an unquestioned divine revelation begun in ancient times, as recorded in the Hebrew scriptures, and culminating with Jesus in the first century CE. But it also raises the profound question of what this revelatory history can and must mean for ongoing human thought and action. The question is vexing and profound because for Kierkegaard it poses the seemingly irresolvable paradox of how the revelation of Jesus as God-Man has then to underlie all that Kierkegaard writes about his own Christian passion, outlook, and practice.

The basis of a whole way of life on an intractable contradiction seems strange indeed, until we reflect that *all supposed divine revelation* supposes the entrance of an infinite, eternal God into the processes of finite, temporal human history. Kierkegaard's firm faith in the deity of the man Jesus and in the redemptive power of that God-Man is a kind of emblem of the paradox of all supposed God-Man encounters and relationships throughout human history, as recounted in the sacred scriptures not only of Christianity but in those of Judaism and Islam as well. Jesus as God-Man may be blasphemy for Jews and Muslims, but divine revelation is as sacred and central to their forms of faith as it is to the Christian's.

And it poses fundamental paradoxes of its own, most notably, how a high and holy, eternal and all-knowing, presumably all-powerful and entirely *self-sufficient* and yet paradoxically *loving* God could be made known to fallible, limited, sin-blinded creatures such as ourselves. In other words, how could the supposed reality of God be translated into the finite, fallible realities of human life, given the assumed *infinite distance* between God and humans?

The answer is usually, "Because God chose to bridge the yawning gap, and what for us may appear impossible is possible for God." But one is bound to wonder how much of this supposed bridging is of human contrivance and how much of divine initiative, and therefore how trustworthy the accounts of divine revelation of truths inaccessible to ordinary human experience and reason are—especially because they must be filtered through human experience and reason in order to be accessible and meaningful to and for humans.

With these thoughts and questions in mind, let us reflect on Kierkegaard's provocative treatments of them in *Philosophical Fragments*, which he alternatively entitles *A Fragment of Philosophy*. I want to concentrate on the role of alleged divine revelation in this book, but I make no attempt at anything resembling an adequate or complete exegesis of it. Kierkegaard wrote numerous challenging books over the course of his life, and it would take at least one huge volume or perhaps many such to even begin to do justice to their contents. There is paradox, irony, tentativeness, and playfulness in all of them, and they are written with a remarkably original and provocative hand. At the heart of all of them, however, is an unquestioned assumption of the momentous reality of divine revelation.

Throughout the *Fragments*, Kierkegaard sets in sharp opposition to one another the Socratic conception of *anamnēsis* or recollection, on the one hand, and the Christian conception of *revelation* or divinely initiated self-disclosure, on the other. Socratic *anamnēsis* is similar to the more familiar contemporary idea of intuition. According to it, already contained somewhere in the back of the mind is the solution to a problem with which one is working, and one has the task of bringing that solution out of unconsciousness into conscious awareness. Socrates did not claim to *teach* the solutions to such problems, only to prod a discussion participant into probing the participant's own mind for the possible answers to questions raised by Socrates as midwife-teacher. Such answers can only be realized personally; they cannot be *taught* in the sense of being handed by teacher to student. But they are capable of being unearthed, "recalled," and resolved by humans within themselves and by means of their own resources.

Divine revelations, on the other hand, provide truths that resonate with the human recipient's thought and awareness, but that could never have been arrived at by the recipient alone—no matter how gifted and discerning the recipient might be. The revelations bridge the abysmal gap between eternity and time, the absolute and relative, the radically unknowable and the knowable or already known, the majesty and dependability of God and the puny incompetencies, numerous uncertainties, limited resources, and plenteous iniquities of the fallible human being.

The revelations render acceptable and believable—although still paradoxical—"the absurdity that the eternal is the historical" (50). In other words, God is in Jesus the Christ and walks about as a human being within a limited period of human history. To know this to be true and to be radically transformed in one's personal life by its existential truth is the supreme miracle and proof of divine revelation.

But there is a problem with this way of thinking about which Kierkegaard is fully aware. What if the bridge of revelation is offered but it, or even its dire existential requirement, cannot be appropriately understood? How can an infinite God successfully communicate God's being, nature, and purposes if there is no way in which fallible humans could appropriate them and strive confidently and meaningfully to live in accordance with them? What if the offered bridge is out of sight or unusable because it is unintelligible to or even seems to be entirely unneeded by mere mortals?

As a convinced Christian, Kierkegaard regards God as a God of intense, unceasing love who yearns for loving concourse, relationship, and intimacy with God's human creatures. How could this possibly be achieved, given the radical differences between God and them? The Christian answer to this fundamental question, as Kierkegaard conceives it, is for God to humble or empty Godself of all God's otherwise incomprehensible majesty, might, and glory and to become a human being among other human beings—to become enfleshed, capable of suffering, susceptible to death, and even in many ways as limited as they are. Such an incarnate deity can be born and die, be appreciated and scorned, experience pleasure and pain, be loved and betrayed, be tempted to sin, undergo intense anxiety and even dreadful doubt about the course of his mission and destiny, writhe in agony on a cross—and so on. In other words, an incarnate God can be truly human without ceasing to be truly God. This is a revelation veiled in paradox.

Kierkegaard's God is the God of the Nicene, Chalcedonian, and Constantinopolitan Creeds of the fourth and fifth centuries CE. He implicitly regards these creeds as conveying the central truths of the Christian tradition. Their ultimate basis lies in such passages of the Christian scriptures as the second chapter of Paul's Epistle to the Philippians, which describes God's momentous decision to be emptied of awesome power and glory, to descend from lofty heaven, and to become a humble participant in human history—and yet remain the one true, loving, and saving God. For later Christian thought, it is not the Father, but the Father's divine Son who descends to earth and becomes incarnate there as Jesus of Nazareth, a distinction that helps to preserve God's place in heaven while yet allowing God to become a real human being on earth.

As such, God is able to share firsthand what it is like to be a human, to be tempted as such, to yearn and pray earnestly in the Garden of Gethsemane for release from his Father's assigned mission of the agony of the cross, to experience doubt, criticism, and rejection by secular and religious authorities, and, with the cry of dereliction on the cross, to know what it is like for a despairing human to feel cut off from and abandoned by God.

Reason raises its head at this point and protests, "But this idea is an irreconcilable paradox and outright contradiction. How could it possibly be believed?" Kierkegaard's answer to this poignant question is that what stands in its way is not so much limited *reason* as human *sin*. The human is created in God's image and should be able to recognize God's presence, even in *kenotic* or radically *emptied* form. When Jesus says that we should love our neighbor even as we love ourselves—and love God with heart, soul, mind, and strength—he has in mind the human as God's creature, made in God's image, and the neighbor as similarly conceived. Like responds to like, and there is fundamental likeness between God and humans given to them at their creation by

God. But the accumulative effects of their sins—and, more pointedly, of their state of radical sinfulness or separation from God—have the effect of defacing and blurring this likeness, even to the point of causing them *not* to recognize God in the startling presence within a period of their own history of the God-Man Jesus the Christ.

How, then, can they come to know him as God's definitive revelation of God's own true, loving, saving self? They surely cannot by mere acts of their wills (50). Their pervasive sinfulness stands stubbornly in the way. If they are ever to become susceptible to really seeing the actuality of God in human form, they must experience removal of the barrier of their state of sinfulness by their complete transformation—in response to Jesus's teaching, ministry, and death on earth, along with his bodily resurrection—into *new beings*. The test of the authenticity of the revelation is its transformative, redeeming, saving effects in each human life, not just the satisfaction of some kind of rational curiosity or need for conceptual clarity. The revelation has the capability of radically transforming us, according to Kierkegaard, where unaided reason or effort never could.

It *becomes* revelation for us by means of its transformative effects on our outlooks and lives. God takes the initiative of enlightening and saving us, making us fully aware of how deeply in need each one of us is of being forgiven for our sins and having the entire orientation and meaning of our lives undergo radical change. It is far from anything we could do unaided and on our own behalf.

At bottom, it is nothing less than a divinely inspired, guided, and shared *miracle*, "the miracle namely, that the eternal condition is given in time" (53). Anything not similarly efficacious and radical would not count for Kierkegaard as something truly revelatory. The miracle is not merely conveyance of information. It is conversion, rebirth, and the redirection and transformation of a formerly sin-ridden, unaware, unloving life. To be radically conquered by the restorative power of God's love is what, for Kierkegaard, constitutes the fundamental significance of the experience of revelation. Apart from it, and the miraculous experience it produces, there would be no true and lasting conviction of or commitment to the reality of God's nature, presence, and power. If God did not reach down to us, we could never find the traction to climb up to him.

This is Kierkegaard's central teaching about the meaning and role of divine revelation. We know that God exists because God has become one of us and our revered teacher and savior in the person of Jesus the Christ. This is the paradoxical scandal of the God-Man or of the eternal God somehow living in the midst and messiness of our human history. Its acceptance into our lives requires a *leap* or *moment* (34, 46–47) made possible by—and only by—the miraculous, unearned, and undeserved *gift* of faith. The reality of God is not for Kierkegaard a speculative problem or concern. It is a deeply religious one, and it turns, for him, on the experienced or experienceable miracle of divine revelation. God makes Godself known to each of us humans—not in general but necessarily to each of us, one-by-one—by God's revelatory action and gracious outreach. This is the beginning and the end of the question of God's existence by Kierkegaard's reckoning.

For him, revelation in the final analysis is intensely personal and cannot be made objective. Its character is irreducibly subjective. The theme of the existential or intensely personal and relentlessly individual character of the experience of divine revelation is developed in chapter 2 of Kierkegaard's lengthy book *Concluding Unscientific Postscript*. The chapter's title is "The Subjective Truth, Inwardness," and the whole book is said to be "unscientific" because it is rooted in revelation and revelatory paradoxes, not mere speculative theory. It has this rootage in common with the earlier work for which it is the intended sequel.

It is interesting to me, paradoxical in its own way, that Kierkegaard writes at enormous length in his many books about what cannot finally be written about or rationally comprehended—only chipped at from many different directions. But his writing is always underlain by his fundamental conviction about the nature and necessity of divine revelation, and the requirement for its subjective appropriation and firsthand experience, on the one hand, and the need for constant emphasis on revelation's inaccessibility to supposedly objective or purely rational, philosophical, or scientific speculation or defense, on the other.

Its significance and truth must be discovered and reaffirmed in the experience of each human life—the experience of rebirth into newness of being, of being miraculously lifted from a state of sin into a new state of divine forgiveness and redemption. This transformative "lifting" is necessary because the state of sin or separation from God is a "sickness unto death," to cite the title and central concern of one of Kierkegaard's books by that title. This new being is made possible, and could only have been made possible by the insertion of the eternal into time, the incarnation of God into the affairs of this world in time. But what about those whose lives preceded the first century, the historical time of God's becoming a human being?

I do not presently have in mind Kierkegaard's answer to this question, but I think it must reside in the paradox of the eternal resident in time. The effects of God's incarnation are not "retroactive" into the past because *retroactive* is a temporal term, and these effects transcend time. They are the miraculous, unthinkable, paradoxical insertion of the eternal into the temporal. The decisive revelation of the God-Man in the first century of the common era is effective and transformative for all persons at all times precisely because it is not temporal but eternal. The mystery of it is essential to its being what, for Kierkegaard, it essentially and eternally is. Apart from mind-wrenching, necessarily paradoxical *revelation*, before which mere human reason pales in significance, there is no existential access to the reality of God's existence and no experience in one's own particular life of the incalculable gift of God's love.

Martin Buber

Nothing could be more obvious to the philosopher-theologian Martin Buber than the existence of God. It requires no argument and indeed resists any and all attempts of argument to prove or make convincing God's existence. The reality of God resides in God's loving initiative and gracious self-disclosure, not in Godward efforts by reasoning, experiencing, or seeking human beings. It resides, in a word, in *revelation*. This is a conviction that he, a convinced Jew, shares with Kierkegaard, a convinced Christian. God for Buber, as for Kierkegaard, is a Person who seeks us out and addresses us, not an object of unassisted human understanding. We encounter God in *relationship* with God, not in even the most earnest speculation about God's existence or nature. And the relationship is initiated by God and sustained by God's love. It is in no sense the outcome of some kind of purely human discernment or unaided human accomplishment.

The revelation of God's character, person, and will is not just some series of one-time events in human history, the effects and meanings of which were in early times inscribed into holy scriptures. Important as earlier accounts of revelation are, they also take place refreshingly and savingly anew when a human being is brought into a genuine relationship with God as a living being, not just as the consequence of the human's ardent aspiration or finally achieved abstract idea.

"God's address to man penetrates the events in all our lives," Buber writes in the afterword to the second edition of *I and Thou*, published in 1957: "and all the events in the world around us, everything biographical and everything historical, and turns it into instruction, into demands for you and me" (182). Revelation, he also states, "is man's emerging from the moment of the supreme encounter being no longer the same as he was when entering into it" (157). His giving great emphasis to the life-transforming power of authentic divine-human encounter and revelation is a point at which Buber's thought chimes in resoundingly with Kierkegaard's conception of the priority and necessity of revelation. Finally, divine revelation is much more than communication of doctrines to be believed or vital information. With revelation, what humans receive "is not a 'content' but a presence, a presence as strength" (158). It is the redeeming presence and strength granted to the relative human person by the "absolute person," God (181).

The crucial point at which the two thinkers depart from one another is the traditional Christian conviction that God's forgiveness of humans for their sins and gift of the transformation of their lives into new being was or is in any way dependent on the death of Jesus on the cross or on the promise of Jesus's claimed resurrection from the dead. For Buber, God's yearning love for God's human creatures is in no way dependent on such a condition. God is ready at all times for the return of each human being into God's presence, relationship, and boundless love. This unceasing emphasis on the need for *return* is for Buber is the unfailing message of the Hebrew prophets, a message that lies at the basis of Jewish faith. Walter Kaufman, the translator and editor of my edition of Buber's *I and Thou*, calls attention to this emphasis in Buber's thought (35–37). The immeasurably holy, eternal, ineffable God longs for communion with God's human creatures. God is a "Thou" seeking lasting relationship with human "thous." Apart from such *lived relationship*, humans have no way of knowing anything trustworthy or reliable about the reality of God or the loving nature of God.

Revelation is lived in relation to the living God or it has no revelatory meaning or saving power. Without it, humans can have no reliable understanding of themselves, their relations to one another, their relations to nonhuman others, or to their world. Buber at one place in his writing presents the world as a kind of circle, the center of which is the living God. Aspects of the world—humans, nonhuman organisms, nonliving features of the world—are each like a radius within the circle that flows from and reaches back to God at its center (148, 163).

All of these aspects of the world are given their existence and significance by the God who exhibits God's reality by their relation to and utter dependence on God. The tree in the forest (57–59), the cat in the home (145), the glance of the wild animal (144), a piece of mica (146–47)—everything in the whole of creation testifies to its relation to God, a relationship without which it would have no existence, function, or meaning.

And this God is not the outcome of abstract speculation but of concrete revelations of and ongoing relationships with God. Everything stems from God, is ultimately created and sustained by God, and points back to God as its ultimate origin and basis. For Buber, revelation makes this idea abundantly convincing, sustaining, and saving in a manner that no amount of independent human reasoning ever could. Does God exist? How could God not exist and human life—or even the universe as a whole—still have purpose, value, and meaning? It, they, we, and I *could not*: this is the conclusion drawn by both Kierkegaard and Buber. For them, the living God is the ground of all that exists, whether living or nonliving—the center of the universe to which all else points, to and from and in relation to which all else derives its distinctive character and particular capability of contribution to the well-being of the whole.

A universe without a personal God, for these two thinkers, the one a Christian and the other a Jew, would be like a wheel without an axle or an old-fashioned clock without its pendulum. It would be inert, inoperative, devoid of value and meaning, and our human lives would be doomed to that same terrible uselessness, absence of direction, and emptiness. The absence of God for them is not just a *conceptual* void; it is a radically *existential* one as well.

Without the presence and strength of the living God made manifest in revelation, the world and all that is in it would become bits of leaf or lint blown without point or purpose into the wind. Divine revelation, Buber asserts, "makes life heavier but heavy with meaning." It is the ultimate, "inexpressible conformation of meaning. It is guaranteed. Nothing, nothing can henceforth be meaningless" (158). Its meaning is none other than the loving presence of God in each human life as well as in and with everything else in God's creation (159). With these ardent claims in mind, accompanied by the similar ones we have seen to be set forth by Kierkegaard, I want us in the final part of this chapter to consider some relevant initial critical comments on the idea that revelation of the sort assumed and described by them is somehow self-evident and self-authenticating, and that it lies beyond the reach of critical examination.

Critical Reflections on Revelation as Self-Confirming

What about the other religions of the world, each with its own kind of revelation or alleged source of saving religious truth? What about those in which a personal God is not the source or central focus and concern of their claimed revelations? Buber mentions and briefly criticizes some of these other religious traditions, such as Advaita Vedanta Hinduism and Hinayana Buddhism (136–41). But he does not directly address the issues raised for his position by their own appeals to revelatory disclosures. In Advaita ("Non-Dualistic") Vedanta, belief in the personality or selfhood of humans or of a God such as Ishvara is taken provisionally into account, but both beliefs are said ultimately to be *maya* or misperception—along with all else in the world of ordinary experience—and only the impersonal Brahman is real. Realization of the reality of Brahman requires transcending or going beyond all thought of human or divine persons, or any kind of I-Thou relations.

Hinayana Buddhism, for its part, regards personality or self as impermanent and unreal—and continuing attachment to it as a cause of radical suffering. Both traditions have their own revelatory experiences conveyed through deep, resolutely disciplined meditational practices, but they are not experiences of a personal God. Then there is Daoism, the ultimate focus of which is the Way of Nature, not a personal God or a class of gods. The problem with the appeal to revelation as the basis of monotheism, therefore, is that *purported revelations are many, and they are not all monotheistic.* In other words, religious revelations are not always thought to be the self-disclosures of a single divine being. Finally, there are the revelations and incarnated avatars of polytheistic religions, such as those in some forms of Hinduism.

Christianity has only one incarnation of God in human form, and for a monotheist like Kierkegaard this one incarnation has decisive significance. But polytheistic Hinduism has many such divine-human incarnations, with many different roles. The religious outlooks I only mention here are clearly different from the monotheistic faiths of Kierkegaard and Buber.

My observations are not intended as disproofs of the revelatory bases of Kierkegaard's Christianity or Buber's Judaism, but only as ways of calling attention to the non-universality or unavoidable plurality of such claimed bases, experiences, and ways of thinking that is exhibited by the undeniable fact if other religious traditions, each with its own kind of ultimate revelatory source, basis, and recourse. The manyness of revelations among the religions of the world, and of the religious faiths of people throughout the world in the past and present, raises serious questions, therefore, about the claimed absolute, unquestionable authority of any one alleged or assumed revelatory source or basis.

Putative revelations cannot be separated from ongoing interpretations of their meanings and alleged truths for each person, tradition, institution, and time. Buber misleads us, therefore, when he argues that the particular kind of revelation or divine disclosure which he takes for granted and to which he constantly appeals "does not wish to be interpreted by us—for that we lack the ability—only to be done by us. . . . The meaning can be received but not experienced; it cannot be experienced, but it can be done, and this is what it intends with us" (159). By "done," I take him to mean, not just carried out in practice, but *obeyed without doubt or question.* This is for me a dangerous assertion, and it is the focus of my second critical reflection on assumptions about revelation made by thinkers like Kierkegaard and Buber.

Why are such assumptions dangerous? For one thing, these two men unquestioningly assume the absolute truth of their own monotheistic way of experiencing, thinking, and acting and set it in implicit opposition to the convictions and claims of all other traditions that differ from this one way. They assume and contend that its truth is *a given* that requires no argument or defense. Paradoxical or even contradictory in some, if not many, ways it might sometimes appear to be, this consequence is only to be expected and never questioned. The words that come immediately to my mind as I reflect on this outlook are *hubris* and *arrogance.*

Clearly, neither Kierkegaard nor Buber intends to be hubristic or arrogant. Both are well aware of the paradoxes, complexities, questions, and uncertainties of their stances of faith and of their personal promulgations of its meanings. They need, however, to be more explicit about the untenability of their claims about revelation's unquestioned absoluteness or supposedly manifest self-authentication for those who do not share their type of religious faith.

Furthermore, not only is a purported revelation meaningless without continuing interpretations of its meanings and applications to the ongoing challenges of life; without such interpretations and applications they can soon lead in wrong and dangerous directions. There is to my mind no such thing as an absolutely binding, true, unquestioned revelation because all supposed revelation has been and must continue to be filtered through human thought and practice, meaning that it has to be interpreted in order to be relevant. And in order to be interpreted, it must be critically questioned and examined at all times and places. To raise doubt or pose critical questions about a claimed revelation and its application to some particular situation is not to exhibit lack of faith in it. It can mean expression of faith in its assumed truth—a faith that may not only withstand doubt but that also requires it.

Absence of such critical reflection can be dangerous, not only because it can put adamant, unquestioning adherents of one religious tradition into serious conflict with one another, as is apparent throughout the many religiously grounded atrocities of human history. It is also dangerous when it becomes a recipe for fanaticism and the cruelties and absurdities that can and frequently have stemmed from it.

The most telling illustration of this observation for me is the chilling story in the Hebrew Bible of Abraham's belief that God had commanded him to slay his own son, Isaac. He raised the knife above his son on the altar and was about to plunge it into his son's breast when an angel stayed his hand. This story is often thought to be evidence of the stalwart, unshakable faith of Abraham in God, and in the sometimes inscrutable will and purposes of God. Kierkegaard spoke in this connection of Abraham as the exemplary, paradoxical, unquestioning "knight of faith" (1941). But I read and interpret the story differently. For me, Abraham should have questioned this supposed divine command or revelation, simply because it made no sense! Perhaps this response would have been the true test of his faith, and it might even have been intended as such by God—a possible and even plausible interpretation of the meaning of the story.

At any rate, to interpret this story in Kierkegaard's manner as possibly endorsing some kind of "teleological suspension of the ethical" required by God in favor of some higher purpose unknown and unknowable at the time to Abraham or any of his peers is an extremely dangerous suggestion. It is such because it preempts one of the most important checks on irrational, fanatical, potentially destructive kinds of claims to faith in God's purposes and will. It substitutes blind faith for reasoned faith—credulous faith in whose name almost any monstrously distorted decision and action could be endorsed.

The true test of Abraham's faith was not his willingness to carry out an absurd command but to scrutinize, question, and reject it as not being of God. It ran against the grain of all that he had previously experienced in relation to God's promise that he would be the father, through his descendants, starting with his son Isaac, of the covenanted people of Israel throughout the ages. This kind of questioning, interpreting, and applying faith is exemplary and commendable in a way that fanatical, unquestioning, blind obedience is not. Neither Kierkegaard nor Buber speaks clearly and relevantly to this crucial point, nor does anyone who insists on the absolute, unquestionable authority of some particular kind of supposed revelation as wholly reliable evidence of the existence, nature, and purposes of God.

Revelation and reason are not opposed. They belong together, each requiring checks on claims to the total competency or sufficiency of the other. Kierkegaard's celebration of the paradoxes of supposed divine revelation as pointers to deeper truths that can only be finally expressed or at least partially grasped in this manner is one thing. It is quite another to read them as not only expectations but celebrations of unreason and absurdity, and he clearly does not intend for them to be viewed in the latter way. However, he also needed, in my judgment, to present them more forcibly and clearly as limits of reason, experience, and interpretation when they have done their best, not as their abrogations.

Another line of criticism of the idea of the absolute, binding authority of supposed revelation is the possibility that Kierkegaard's and Buber's faith in a personal deity is just a projection of humanity onto the heavens. Not only are humans said in monotheistic forms of religious faith to be made in the image of God. We must not overlook the possibility that the idea of a distinct, personal, single God of the universe and of all things human is *made in the image of human beings*. It is possibly not so much revealed as unconsciously imagined in a manner that carries with it the long-assumed dominance of humans over the whole of nature and even their not being mere creatures of nature—another kind of treacherous anthropomorphism. We will take up this pertinent line of criticism in the next chapter when we discuss the challenging ideas of Ludwig Feuerbach.

Conclusion

Kierkegaard and Buber do masterful jobs of developing and defending interpretations of Christianity, on the one hand, and Judaism, on the other—interpretations that turn crucially on their unshakable convictions about the reality of God and of God's gracious, saving revelations to human beings. But of course their interpretations differ in some crucial respects, most notably in their radically different responses to the significance of the gospel accounts of the life, death, and resurrection from the dead of Jesus of Nazareth. These differences bring into clear focus the fact that purported divine revelations are not entirely self-authenticating or beyond question. Not only are they originally communicated by human beings to other human beings, but their significance must be interpreted by humans and applied by humans to ever-emerging and ever-changing circumstances and times. This fact brings into serious question, therefore, any claim to the absolute, unquestionable, incontrovertible authority of any sort of acclaimed divine revelation.

What Kierkegaard and Buber, or any other interpreters of alleged revelation, may take for granted as constituting divine revelation is always open to honest, earnest questioning and doubting. The evidence of such questioning and doubting through the two millennia of the Common Era is a sign of the seriousness with which purported revelations of God's holy presence, purpose, and will have been taken from the times of their earliest presentations. An alleged divine revelation worthy of attention is one that *requires* the deepest and most persistent kinds of ongoing interpretation of its meanings for the lives of human individuals, for their relations with one another, and for their responsible roles in relation to the ecosystems of the earth and their innumerable but presently gravely imperiled forms of life.

We can be grateful for the claims about revelations and the provocative interpretations of their meanings Kierkegaard, Buber, and the prophets, saints, theologians, writers, and teachers throughout human history have offered for our consideration. But we are not only *entitled* to raise questions about their assumptions, reasonings, and interpretations, but *obligated* to do so in order to appropriate into our own lives whatever wisdom we can discern and share with one another as being present there. Such interpretations may and will differ, but such differences can enrich rather than detract from what each such interpreter has ardently to claim about religious truth.

Different interpretations by competent and responsible interpreters can testify to profound and even inexhaustible meanings in many different claimed disclosures of religious truths rather than casting into final doubt and consequent wholesale dismissal all such alleged meanings—and with them the whole field of religious experience and thought. We will want to keep this reminder in our consciousness as we turn in the next chapter to critical questions relating to traditional theism brought to the fore and developed at impressive length by Feuerbach.

Chapter Two

God as the Projected Image of Man

The nineteenth-century German philosopher Ludwig Feuerbach offers at one place in his seminal work, *The Essence of Christianity*, this summary statement of the view of God that he posits and defends throughout the work:

> God as an extramundane being is, however, nothing else than the nature of man withdrawn from the world and concentrated in itself, freed from all worldly ties and entanglements, and positing itself in this condition as a real objective being, or nothing else than the consciousness of the power to abstract oneself from all that is external, and to live for and with oneself alone, under the form which this power takes in religion, namely, that of a being distinct, apart from man. (2008, 56)

God, for Feuerbach, is therefore nothing other than a human being radically abstracted and writ large, a solitary and entirely self-sufficient being requiring nothing other than itself to exist.

God is, in other words, a projection of human subjectivity, imagination, and yearning that accords to this subjective projection the exalted status of an objective divine being. The austere self-sufficiency of such an imagined being is supplemented, however, with the ideal of love, an ideal abstractly instantiated in the Christian anthropomorphized God by the idea that God has a triune nature. God is not only Father but also Son, and God loves his Son, even as the Son loves the Father. "The third person in the Trinity," namely the Holy Spirit, Feuerbach writes, "expresses nothing further than the love of the two divine persons towards each other" and of these two divine persons toward human beings (57). What has been initially apotheosized or raised up from human experience and life, therefore, returns back to them as their loving, saving God in the Christian tradition as Feuerbach conceives its origin and nature.

God does not actually or objectively exist, in this view. God's supposed existence and nature are the products of human imagination, of conceiving God in the image of humans and subsequently of humans in the image of God. What binds these two together is the intense human need for acceptance, forgiveness, love, and existential meaning. The archetype of divine love is derived from the overwhelming human need to love and to be loved in return. The essence of the Christian religion, for Feuerbach, lies here. It is the mundane, natural, hopeful, and originally entirely *human* person projected into the high heavens as the infinitely exalted and holy *divine* Person.

His interpretation of Christian faith, and implicitly and ultimately for him of all types of monotheistic religious faith, should not be dismissed out of hand by committed monotheists. Feuerbach devotes numerous pages of rational analysis and argument to the clarification and defense of his interpretation that are well worthy of consideration by them. We can set these pages in contrast to Kierkegaard's and Buber's appeals to divine *revelation* as the origin of true religion, this alleged origin assumed by them to lie in the initiative of the one true God rather than in the speculations, aspirations, hopes, and needs of fallible human beings.

The contrast can help to stimulate our imaginations and critical thinking as we continue to contemplate arguments in support of, and those critical of, monotheism. I begin this chapter with exposition and critical interpretation of Feuerbach's conception of religious *revelation*. It is fitting that I do so, given the principal focus of both Kierkegaard and Buber, discussed in the preceding chapter, on the absolute authority of divine revelation or gracious loving, forgiving, and empowering divine self-disclosure—seen by them as the unquestionable foundation of their respective forms of religious faith.

Revelation and the Religious Commitment
to One Personal God

In the previous chapter, I called attention to three major problems with an unquestioning appeal to the absolute authority of any particular claimed revelation of religious truth. The first one is that claimed definitive and binding revelations are many. This fact can be clearly discerned in the differences, and not just the similarities, among Judaism, Christianity, and Islam. The three make ultimate appeal to a single personal deity and the choices of that deity to make itself known to humankind. But the contents of their respective revelations do not agree in all aspects, and the differences among them are in some senses major, and not just minor.

This fact becomes even more evident when it comes to nonthe-istic or non-monotheistic religions such as Advaita Vedanta Hinduism, Hinayana Buddhism, Polytheistic Hinduism, and Daoism—religions that do not have as their ultimate focus a single personal deity. But such religions do have their own kinds of revelation or intensely informative, empowering revelatory experiences, meaning not only that revelations are many in the religions of the world, but that what counts as revelation is different among them.

The Buddha, for example, discovered and founded what became his religious tradition by a sudden awakening after years of searching and meditating. He, and not some sort of God, took the initiative and underwent the long discipline that finally led to this awakening. Simi-larly, in Advaita Vedanta Hinduism, the religious ultimate, Brahman, is confirmed as such via meditation, not by any kind of divine initiative, and Brahman is regarded, not as *a being*, in a manner similar to the theistic religions, where God relates to innumerable other beings in the world God has created, but as the *sole Reality*. Revelation as experienced disclosure of ultimate religious truth is the basis of these two religious outlooks, but such disclosure is not initiated by a personal deity.

The second problem with an appeal to the absoluteness of any particular kind of revelation or experiential basis in a particular religion is that it can sometimes become extremely dangerous. It is so when, as with Kierkegaard in particular, the revelation is expected to be pervasively paradoxical and even self-contradictory because its divine origin is so far above and beyond anything approaching human comprehension. When a purported revelation is shielded in this manner from deeply probing doubt and questioning, it can—at least in principle—allow anything or at least almost anything to be permitted and commanded by it.

I used the biblical example of Abraham's belief that God commanded him to slay his own son to make this point. As I interpret this story, Abraham should have questioned and critically interpreted the putative revelation, not blindly acted in accordance with it. This would, in my view, have been the proper test of his faith in God. Blind, unwavering, unquestioning assent to the supposed divine command was not. A purported revelation is a starting point, not a stopping point of inquiry, a kind of weighty hypothesis to be tested reverently but also critically for its reliability and truth. To treat it in this manner is entirely consistent with its supposed divine origin.

The third criticism I mounted against unquestioning appeals to revelation, to assumed sources of religious faith from which a particular form of faith is said to flow, and which is claimed to be absolute and beyond question, applies especially to monotheistic forms of faith but also in a deep sense to most kinds of religious tradition. This criticism focuses on the suspicion that all appeals to supernatural origins of religious truth are, when properly understood, the results of finite human experience, thought, and imagination. And they cannot help but be couched in such terms in order to be intelligible and applicable to human life. As such, they are open to and in need of critical questioning and interpretation at all times. To be truly receptive to revelation is to search critically for its meanings.

Revelations do not stem exclusively, in other words, from some realm above or beyond this world or in a manner transcending mundane, even if deeply influential and far-ranging, human speculations and beliefs. Seen in this way, revelation is crucially dependent on human thought and experience even when these factors are not regarded as its ultimate source. It is such even when it stems from outstanding *eureka* moments or profound special awakenings of such thought and experience. There is no defensible way in which the *human part* of supposed divine-human encounters can or should be ignored or fail to be taken into account.

This idea is the key to Feuerbach's interpretation of the role of so-called revelations in religions, and particularly in the religion to which he devotes his principal attention in his appropriately entitled book *The Essence of Christianity.* I turn first, then, to his analysis of the long-held idea of religious revelation as the unquestionable, supernatural basis of religious conviction, belief, and action. This analysis contains much to stimulate our critical reflection, even though it does not exhaust the possible meanings of revelation as a principal factor in religious thought.

Feuerbach's Critique of Revelation as the Basis of Religious Commitment

According to Feuerbach, revelation is not the unequivocal origin and binding basis of a particular kind of religious faith, contrary to the frequent protestations of its adherents. It is not such and cannot be such because it is the outcome in all religions, and most particularly in the Christian one of human imagination and human projection. God for him is not an independently existing, wholly unique Divine Person but an extremely magnified, highly abstracted human one, and God's supposed revelations to human beings are like boomerangs thrown out *by them* and predictably returning circuitously *to them* (2008, 171). How does Feuerbach go about defending this radical idea—radical, at least, when compared to traditional religious thought, especially in monotheistic religious traditions such as the Christian one?

One of his arguments in defense of this idea is that God, in order to communicate successively, meaningfully, and transformatively to human beings, has no other recourse than to couch revelation into forms that can be meaningful to them. Were God to try to reveal Godself as allegedly existing in God's own character and right, the intended revelation would fail to disclose anything intelligible to human beings. In other words, it would fail entirely to be a revelation. From this line of reasoning, Feuerbach draws the following conclusion: "The contents of the divine revelation are of human origin, for they have proceeded not from God as God, but from God as determined by human reason, human wants, that is, directly from human reason and human wants. . . . Here we have a striking confirmation of the position that the secret of theology is nothing else than anthropology—the knowledge of God nothing else than a knowledge of man!" (171). Consistently with what he reasons to be the human origin of all alleged divine revelations, Feuerbach draws the additional conclusion that all claims to divine revelation must be kept open to human investigation, questioning, and critical scrutiny. No alleged revelation, even of that thought to reside in the pages of the Bible or other sacred writings, can be simply taken for granted as such. To regard a historical book like the Bible, "necessarily subject to all the conditions of a temporal, finite production . . . as an eternal, absolute, universally authoritative word, is—superstition and sophistry" (173). It is also, I might add, a possible recipe for blind, unthinking fanaticism.

The very human and entirely necessary need to critically question, interpret, and apply the pages of the biblical text to daily life for the sake of arriving at intelligible beliefs and defensible practices—to say nothing of the requirement to prioritize some of its passages over others in order to make sense of its meanings as a whole—inevitably inserts the hand of the human into the putative revelatory text. A religious text would be meaningless without continuing conscientious interpretations of its implicit lessons for thought and life, and these interpretive acts, even in their most competent and convincing versions, are acts of fallible human beings.

Such judicious and often eloquent expositors and defenders of sacred texts as Kierkegaard and Buber did not and could not shrink from this necessary task, which the alleged divine comes inevitably to be mixed in with the finite and fallible human. This observation does not in itself deny the Bible's or any other sacred text's revelatory significance, but it does remove from it claims to its absolute, unquestionable authority. It also reminds us that the biblical texts came to be written in times quite different from our times in many crucial respects, and are thus in constant need of exploring convincing ways to bridge the considerable distance extending from those early times to our own.

We should not fail to take into account the possibility that what might have seemed to make perfect good sense or to be entirely absent at one time may no longer be so in either of these two senses at a later one. Examples would be such things in the first century of the Common

Era as gods and goddesses incarnated in human form, routine cases of demon possession, an earth-centered universe, and the absence of natural science and technology as we conceive and make routine use of them today. History, after all, mixes novelty with continuity, as does even the passage of one moment of time to the next. Each new moment is precisely that—*new*—even if only in recognition of its distinction from the preceding moment. And successive epochs of history combine aspects of change, sometimes substantial, previously unpredictable, or even formerly inconceivable change, with continuities inherited from the past. An alleged revelation that is claimed to be impervious to change and in no need of reconsidered applications to changing times, *even over thousands of years*, is in danger of soon becoming obsolete and irrelevant, at least in highly significant respects.

Appeals to the absolute and infallible truths of a claimed divinely revealed sacred text and/or tradition can also be serious threats to any democratic social order by failing to acknowledge this claim as issuing from fallible human judgments about the history and nature of the text, as well as the fallibility of those who claim to offer equally infallible, unquestionable interpretations of its current meanings and applications. This approach and attitude can be sources of serious disruption and threat to the public weal, as is evident in the dogmatic, so-called White Christian Nationalism in today's United States. Alleged absolutes of any kind, including those of this kind do not respect or allow for meaningful debate among proponents of different views of public policy. A theocratic state is not really the rule of God, as its name signifies. It is in reality the rule of rank pretenders to absolute, alleged scripturally warranted divine authority, whether the scripture in question be those of the Hebrew Bible, the Christian Bible, or the Islamic Qur'an.

Feuerbach's contention that claims to the existence of God are nothing more than anthropomorphic projections are not self-evidentially true, but they do pose a possibility that needs to be taken into consideration—at least generally, if not down to their every finite detail. And he is entirely right, in my judgment, that to claim the absolute, timeless, unquestionable authority of any kind of purported revelation would be a serious and irresponsible mistake. Revelation cannot stand alone as the basis of religious faith. Its meanings must be constantly subjected to critical questioning and interpretation if they are to be made relevant to the lives of human beings in their continuing but also changing histories.

To *question* their meanings is entirely consistent with *reverencing* them—it is, in fact, required by appropriate and continual testing of their contents. Kierkegaard, who gives every indication of unquestioning assent to major themes of traditional Christian faith, calls our attention to what he appropriately regards as the final crucial test of any alleged religious revelation, namely, its power to guide and transform human life in religiously enriching, morally laudable, and culturally meaningful ways—and to do so in every passing age. A revelation that cannot meet this existential test would not qualify as an authentic revelation of the sacred or holy, and Kierkegaard is right to insist on the test's religious importance.

But there are debatable *conceptual* aspects of putative revelations as well that must also be taken into critical account, and Feuerbach devotes considerable attention to many pertinent ones of these. My focus in this book is on Middle Eastern and Western forms of monotheism, but it also applies—appropriate changes of characterization and description having been made—to Eastern ones as well.

The first conceptual aspect of traditional monotheism to be discussed here, now that we have inquired into Feuerbach's critically important view of revelation, is God's relation to nature. The second is the general view of God as conceived in traditional Middle Eastern and Western monotheism. The third is the more particular conception of God in Trinitarian Christianity. In each of these respects, Feuerbach provides an analysis of the origins of such ideas and argues against their plausibility. His analysis also serves as a fitting warning against the idea that that appeals to the authority of allegedly infallible divine revelation can be ensured only by docile responses of unquestioning faith. What is said to lie beyond the province of inquiring, questioning, dialogical reasoning can hardly be defended as reasonable.

The public, and not just private, significance of this observation should be apparent to all. Authoritarian regimes, and especially those of an alleged theocratic character, have the well-deserved and deplorable historical reputation of repressive ones, hopelessly out of touch with the needs and concerns of the majority of their people. The so-called divine right of kings and the alleged absolute authority of their monarchy and rule is a pertinent example. Authoritarian absolutism of any kind, secular or religious, is the formidable enemy of civil discourse, personal freedom, and any stable and just social, religious, or political order.

In the final section of this chapter, I shall weigh the significance of these arguments for religious faith in today's world and in this way set the scene for the religious thinker whose thought will be interpreted, analyzed, and evaluated in chapter three, namely, the Protestant theologian Paul Tillich.

God's Relation to Nature

What is God's relation to nature? For Feuerbach, the traditional conception of God allows no meaningful answer to this question. For example, God is said to have created the material universe, but denied to him is the use of any determinate activity or means to do so. In the Book of Genesis, God broods on the watery deep or chaos and transforms it into a world. God does not create the world out of nothing in that scriptural text but out of something, a something that has the *potential* to become a world. But the latter idea became unsatisfactory over time because it was seen as a limitation of God's creative power. God's power is unlimited and therefore not dependent on any kind of preexisting material factors or means, or any kind of commonality of character with such. God must therefore be regarded as wholly immaterial pure spirit and yet somehow—even if only incomprehensively so—as creator of the material world.

So God must be immaterial, without any sort of embodiment, and God must therefore create the world ex nihilo, that is, out of nothing. How a purely spiritual God could create a pervasively material world out of nothing is given no explanation because it defies all that humans can possibly conceive as acts of production, enactment, or creation. All of our making is making something out of something. All of our creations are transformations of something already existent. Divine creation of the world is therefore absurd, an incomprehensible activity, but it is assumed to be such because of the assumption that God cannot be limited or qualified by anything other than God. God is therefore radically unrestricted by anything external to God (178–83).

Furthermore, God's continuing support of the world, to say nothing of any intelligible account of God's particular relationships with the world, is rendered moot. A God absolutely different from this existing world can neither create the world, be involved in its affairs, or speak in any manner to the needs and concerns of human beings. An absolutely, infinitely different God is an absolutely *irrelevant* God, a God who could have no concourse of any kind with any aspect of the world or its inhabitants. Of what religious interest could such a God be?

The typical religious answer to this kind of question is the one to which Kierkegaard gives the repeated response, as we have seen, that we should expect matters having to do with God and God's assumed creation of the world and of things relating to the world to be paradoxical, contradictory, and ultimately unintelligible in at least some important ways. But a dependable revelation tells us that they must be so, and we should therefore accept and believe them. Our lives can be radically transformed by them, as Kierkegaard insists, so they are *pragmatically* justified even though they are *conceptually* unintelligible.

The question left hanging by such a familiar response among many theists, however, is how can we go about believing and committing to something that is admittedly conceptually inconceivable?. How can we choose to believe something that makes no sense? It is one thing to leave room for mystery; this is assuredly needed. But to make *everything* about God's creation, sustenance, and relation to the world an insoluble conundrum is to make religion and fundamental religious assertions inaccessible by implication, locked away from thoughtful interpretation or meaningful acceptance. One can only *pretend* to believe in and be committed to something that is admittedly incomprehensible—meaning that all such profession of belief is nothing at bottom but pretension.

If God is totally different from the world, God could have no concourse with or relation to it or to any of its creatures, including humans. Only a humanly projected, humanlike God can be a meaningful and relevant God, according to Feuerbach. This is why traits like *loving, just, merciful, gracious, trustworthy, saving,* and the like are attributed to God. A God totally unlike anything in nature or human beings would be a totally detached, unknowable, irrelevant God. He develops this point in greater detail, as we shall see in the next two sections.

The Monotheistic Conception of God

We saw in the previous section that for God to be related to the world, God cannot be totally other than the world. The point applies to supposed divine revelation, divine creation of the world, and God's concern about and care for the world. Therefore, a God of such supposed absolutes as omniscience, omnipresence, and omnipotence, and omnibenevolence would have to separate God from any kind of meaningful connections to the finite, nonabsolute world and its creatures.

A God who already knows everything that can be known and who lives outside of time would be a God who knows to the finest detail everything I can know or experience, including my most inward and private thoughts. This means that I have no privacy or inwardness of my own, and thus, no ultimate individuality or uniqueness of my own. All that I think, know, wonder about, imagine, plan, etc. is immediately evident in fine detail to God. What may take time for me, and sometimes a lot of time for me, is immediate to a timeless God. What in the future is dark, unpredictable, and unknown for me is an infinite present for God. What I may long have forgotten is retained in God because God has no dependence either on memory or anticipation for God's absolute knowledge.

What may feel like genuine freedom of thought and action in the face of an unknown future is nothing more than an instantaneous, all-encompassing, unchanging, wholly apprehended *Now* for God. Analogous to a machine that has mastered all of the possible moves in a game and can accurately play out every move and its consequences, what seems to me to be subject to my free decisions is for God already known and predetermined. It could not be otherwise, or so the reasoning goes, if God is to be absolute in every possible respect in order to be recognized and worshipped as the one true God.

In God's eyes, I can only be seen as a robot, not truly as a person. And God is an Orwellian, police-state God, not a God who can respect my independence and privacy. And I am like the piece on a chessboard who thinks of itself as indeterminate or free but cannot truly be such because God knows all and controls all. The only recourse to this outcome is to think of God as a human projection or creation and, as such, being limited and finite in at least some crucial respects.

Once the *quantitative* differences between God and humans become qualitative—and we give to God such attributes as omnipotence, omniscience, omnipresence, nontemporality, immateriality (or pure spirituality), creator of the world out of nothing, and the like—God becomes unknowable and completely out of touch with everything in the world. This is so even though all such omni-attributes are nothing more than extrapolations from human sensate experience (Feuerbach 176–77).

A finite, limited, human-like monotheistic God may sound like something different from what soon became the traditional monotheistic view of God, but it is the only conception able to save God from incomprehensibility and irrelevance. This is Feuerbach's main conclusion. Only a God who is fundamentally similar to humans qualitatively and not just quantitatively, is a God worthy of recognition as such by human worshippers. But implicit in this recognition for Feuerbach is that God is no more, in the final analysis, than a human projection. The idea of an absolute, unprojected, finally definitive, comprehensible, and convincing revelatory experience of the existence and providential love and care of such a God is thus for him an illusion. This mention of divine love and care brings us to Feuerbach's interpretation of the Christian doctrine of God as a *Trinity*, even while continuing to be conceived as the *One* true God.

The Trinitarian View of God

We saw in chapter one that Kierkegaard regards the traditional Christian portrayal of Jesus of Nazareth as the God-man to be a contradiction, but a contradiction that, once believed in and ardently committed to, becomes the basis for release from the hopeless sinful state of humans and their transformation into radical newness of life. Apart from such contradiction or paradox, there is for him no salvation. But behind this contradiction of reason, there is another, still more fundamental one for Kierkegaard. This the mystery of God as one and yet as three, the doctrine of the Trinity.

Feuerbach argues that monotheistic reason or rational faith in the one true God requires that there be only one God. But the active human imagination, in order to account for the idea that God has an only begotten Son who can descend to earth and die on the cross in order to satisfy the demand of divine justice by appropriate punishment entailed by the universal fall of humans into sin, requires that the Son also be God. It must be God who dies but also God who is eternal or everlasting who dies. The contradiction of the God-Man for Feuerbach thus points to the contradiction of the God who is somehow Three and yet One, whose love results in his willingness to suffer and die on behalf of humankind, but whose immortal nature also makes inevitable his physical resurrection from the dead in the first century CE.

Reason understandably rejects this idea, while imagination demands and therefore accepts it. What is demanded is a contradiction. Feuerbach summarizes the contradiction in this way: "The idea of the Trinity demands that man should think the opposite of what he imagines, and imagine the opposite of what he thinks [or reasons]—that he should think phantoms realities" (191; the square brackets are mine). The so-called three realities are phantoms for him because a personal God must be one substance, but the Trinity requires three substances because there can be no substantial single personality somehow divisible into three substances.

Unlike Kierkegaard, Feuerbach is not tolerant of radical religious paradoxes such as this. God is supposed, on the one hand, to be personal, as humans are personal. God is not an abstraction but a real being. But on the other hand, God is made something abstract and unintelligible by the doctrine of the Trinity that is so essential to traditional Christianity. The incarnation makes God a human being, and this idea in itself shows the idea of God, and especially the idea of God as a distinct humanlike person, to be inevitable.

But it is inevitable, in the final analysis, as a projection of humanity—the projection of a being similar in critical respects to humans and yet paradoxically absolutized into something nonhuman—a finite person first made into an infinite one and then become finite again in the person of Jesus. The boomerang thrown out into a supernatural realm by humans comes back to them with the supposed Son of God's incarnation in the natural realm. The idea of the Holy Spirit, as the third personal aspect of the Trinity, continues this ongoing boomerang effect in Feuerbach's thinking.

The Holy Spirit is God with us, God continuing to love, protect, and save us, while still being the maker of heaven and earth and our incarnate friend. What is holy, saving, awesome mystery for traditional Christianity is for Feuerbach meaningless absurdity. And no less absurd for him is monotheism of all kinds, Trinitarian—as with Søren Kierkegaard—and unqualifiedly monotheistic, as with Martin Buber. For Feuerbach, there is no convincing way to convert a fallible human projection into an existent divine reality. What goes around comes back around, essentially unchanged.

Critical Reflections

A religious outlook like that of Martin Buber and Søren Kierkegaard seems to go something like this: there is in fact a being such as God who has created the universe and its ongoing processes and evolutions, including the evolution of human beings. God has intense love for these humans and wants them to love their creator God in return. God therefore reaches down to them and reveals this divine love to them, promising them its saving presence and power. But so great is the distance between God and man that this revelation, in order to be truly that, must be contained in terms and experiences that are at least partly intelligible to finite human persons. The term *partial* is crucial. Humans will be able to understand enough of the revelation to recognize its authority, commit to its explicit and implicit systems of thought, and incorporate it into their lives.

When they are receptive and willing enough to do so, they will experience a transformative loving and saving relationship with God. But there will also be many aspects of God's nature and loving relationship that they will not be able to understand, no matter how hard they try, in view of the vast differences between their nature's and God's. So the revelation will be paradoxical and unintelligible in many respects while also clear enough to produce its miraculous transformative effects.

Its clarity will incorporate features intelligible to human beings, so it will of course have conceptions, stories, and ways of thinking that are clear *to them*. In a word, it will have an essential, ineliminable *anthropomorphic* character. But it will also be replete with warnings and reminders that, while there are analogies between God and humans, these anthropocentric features are *only* analogies, metaphors, and suggestions, and not *literal* likenesses. As such, they will require expression in nondiscursive ways such as paradox, symbol, myth, rite, and story.

Thus, when Feuerbach takes Christianity to task for essential aspects of it which do not admit of clear statement or a content entirely analyzable and perspicuous to the rational mind, this fact is only to be expected. Christianity's anthropomorphic character in particular is necessary because it expresses a genuine relationship established by God with human beings, a relationship that by its very nature can only partially bridge the enormous gulf between God's and their modes of existence.

Let me use an analogy to try to get at this idea regarding divine-human revelation and relationship. Let's say that a physician, after examining and analyzing a condition of ill health I am suffering from, tells me that unfortunately I have a particularly rare and extremely complex disease. But then she goes on to assure me that there is a recently discovered cure for the disease, and that she would like to use it as the treatment for me. I ask her to explain the possible cure, and she proceeds to do so. I soon halt her in the process and complain that she has lost me. There is too much in her reasoning and in her unfamiliar medical jargon I cannot comprehend or even pronounce.

My doctor than patiently tries to communicate the nature of my disease and its possible cure in terms that I might better understand. She succeeds to some extent but also warns me that, in order fully to comprehend what she is trying to explain, I would need to have extensive training as a medical researcher in a particular field. My doctor is like the human recipient and conveyer of a divine revelation. The revelation recipient is quick to remind us that this is how it came to the recipient, and that the recipient is handing it on to us without even the recipient's own complete understanding of its import. In other words, a completely intelligible, transparently clear revelation from the one true God could in no way qualify as such for fallible human beings! But at the same time, it has to be intelligible enough to qualify as a revelation, namely, a disclosure of vitally important meanings and truths from God to humans.

Without revelation, there are no definitive truths about God. With revelation, these truths can only be partial and to a significant extent rationally unclear—in other words, weighted with paradox and even marked in significant degree by what may look like outright contradiction. This is the logic of revealed religion as represented in the monotheistic religions of Judaism, Christianity, and Islam—and this logic is insisted on by Kierkegaard and Buber. It is a logic that is opaque and unconvincing to Feuerbach because he demands pervasive conceptual conviction and clarity in any putative revelation. He appears to have no patience with supposed revelatory paradox and contradiction.

A lot of the difference between him and the two monotheists centers on the concept of *faith*. There is faith seeking understanding: call it *reasoning faith*, and faith accepting necessary limitations of understanding: call it *faithful reasoning*. The first requires that religious faith be as intelligible and reasonable as possible. The second recognizes the limitations of reason when it comes to thinking about God and puts its trust in areas of thought, experience, and practice that reason is not competent fully to understand. These two aspects of religious faith are in necessary tension with one another because religion is not just something to be abstractly thought about but also something to be concretely lived. But it cannot be meaningfully lived without the continuing effort and aspiration of thought. Reasoning faith and faithful reasoning go necessarily together.

I do not mean these comments to be understood as defenses of monotheism, whether based primarily on reason or on revelation. I mean them here just to show how Kierkegaard and Buber, on the one hand, and Feuerbach on the other, can be seen as two sides of the religious coin. If either side is carried to an extreme, then the other will be lost sight of. If I am not grasped and transformed by something unexpected, unmanageable, and revelatory, I can hardly claim to be faithfully religious.

But if I fail to think persistently and as clearly as possible about the meaning of putative revelatory experiences—accepting and obeying them as such in a spirit of blind credulity—then I am in grave danger of stumbling into the pit of fanaticism, as in the case of Abraham thinking that God commanded Abraham to kill his own son—the son of previous divinely bestowed covenant and promise. In other words, *I have failed to be reasonably faithful.* Flat contradiction is not commended by meaningful religious faith. Reason and faith are complements to and not enemies of one another in this way of thinking.

There are admitted paradoxes and seeming contradictions in what may count as authentic revelations, but the second-century Church Father Tertullian's famous dictum, *credo quia absurdum,* "I believe because it is absurd," must be rejected out of hand. A pervasively absurd, completely incomprehensible revelation would be *no revelation* in any sense of the term. And it could soon become a recipe for unmitigated disaster. Feuerbach is well within his rights in insisting at least on this crucial point.

But he perhaps veers too far in the rationalistic direction at the expense of a view of authentic religious revelation as a necessary blend of the clearly and unmistakably rational, on the one hand, and the mysterious and only partly articulable by exclusively rational modes of thought and discourse, on the other. Religious experience, more often than not, may put us in touch with realities and truths that have a logic and rationality of their own—ones that reason alone, or strictly rational approaches by themselves, are not entirely competent to discover, articulate, or confirm.

We need to keep an open mind about this possibility while still respecting in high measure Feuerbach's insistence on the critical role of rationality and good sense in religious thought. Religious faith and competent reason should not be set in either-or competition with one another but as standing in a proper both-and relationship with one another. This idea is easy enough to state, but it is not at all easy to maintain, especially in the domain of religion. The one is always in danger of being given exclusive attention and emphasis at the expense of the other.

Conclusion

In this chapter, I have set the philosopher Ludwig Feuerbach in opposition to two highly esteemed monotheistic thinkers, Søren Kierkegaard and Martin Buber—Feuerbach a rational critic of monotheism, claiming that it is nothing more, in the final analysis, than an imagined and projected human being or human-like figure onto the heavens, and the second two affirming and welcoming what they regard as authentic revelations of the one truly existent God. The contrast between Feuerbach and the other two thinkers helps us, in my view, to think in clarifying ways about their respective perspectives on monotheism, including both their possible similarities and their differences. It helps us especially, in my view, to think both critically and constructively about the idea of *revelations* of the sacred—an idea that is crucial in many forms and in many ways to at least most kinds of religious experience, expression, and practice.

Before leaving this chapter, I want to remind the reader that the monotheism that is the critical focus of the present book is that of Judaism, Christianity, and Islam. I do not claim that its purview includes monotheism of all types. Showing that to be so would be a much larger task than the one I have embarked upon here.

In the next chapter, we will reflect on the novel and in many ways illuminating and challenging statements, analyses, and arguments of the German Protestant theologian-philosopher Paul Tillich, who came to the shores of the United States in the early 1930s after being removed from his university teaching position by order of the Nazi state. His social-political views, in particular, were judged to be too controversial and too out of accord with those heralded by the new Fascist regime. Tillich gives us perspectives on revelation, God, Christian thought, and Christian life that are different in important regards from those of Kierkegaard and Feuerbach.

Chapter Three

The God Above God

The principal focus of this chapter is Paul Tillich's concept of God. According to him, *existence* is a limited and limiting category and cannot, therefore, be applied to God. Instead of thinking of God as an existent being among other existent beings, we must think of God as Being-Itself, the presence, power, motivation, and support that lies behind and gives to all types of existent beings the ability to persevere in the face of the formidable threats, uncertainties, anxieties, and failures that mark their finite natures as individuals and their collective dependencies and relationships.

Especially in the case of human beings, Tillich argues in his book *The Courage to Be* that Being-Itself strengthens and empowers their lives, giving to them a capability of confident self-affirmation, as well as constant hope of renewal despite (1) their moral failures, (2) the harrowing threat of contingent accidents accompanied by the surety of their future deaths, and (3) their experiences of emptiness or failures to find ultimate, sustaining purpose, value, and meaning in their lives. For Tillich these are the three major forms of existential anxiety, and all humans, as finite beings, are heir to them. Apart from the presence and power of Being-Itself, the ground of their finite existence and of all finite forms of existence, humans would be in grave jeopardy of wholesale moral self-condemnation, ineradicable anxiety about an always uncertain future and their approaching death, and bleak meaninglessness and despair (1952, 40–57).

In the following passage from the first volume of his three-volume *Systematic Theology*, Tillich shows why, for him, God cannot be a finite, particular, personal, or even *existent* Being in any literal sense of those terms—no matter how greatly magnified or exalted the meanings of such terms might be assumed to have when applied to God: "Selfhood, individuality, dynamics, and freedom all include manifoldness, definiteness, differentiation, and limitation. To be something is not to be something else. To be here and now in the process of becoming is not to be there and then. All categories of thought and reality express this situation. To be something is to be finite" (1951, 190). In other words, since God is the ultimate source and support of all that exists, God cannot be *a* Being among other beings.

God's absolute distinction from all existing entities, including human beings, shows God unmistakably to be none other than Being-Itself and, as such, the ontological ground of all that ever has been or that ever will exist. As Being-Itself, God is undoubtedly *real* but not merely *existent*. Existence, which is invariably *finite*, presupposes God or Being-Itself as its *infinite* ground.

It is ironic to reflect that many of the arguments presented by Ludwig Feuerbach to show that the idea of a personal God is nothing more than an anthropomorphic projection would be acceptable to Tillich because they reveal a confusion of the finite with the infinite—of a supposedly single, personal divine being with Being-Itself, which is for Tillich the only conceivable true God. For both of these thinkers, professed belief in a literal personal God is a grave mistake. Atheism is even defended and recommended by both of them, if by *atheism* is meant rejection of the traditional conception of God as a distinct personal being among other beings. Left hanging by this observation, however, is how Tillich can continue to be commonly regarded, and to confidently regard himself, as a *Christian theologian*.

How can Tillich be a serious practicing theologian throughout his life and continue to deny the existence of a personal God? How can he continue to be a Christian for whom the personality and distinctive existence of God—a God who, for traditional Jews as well as Christians, lovingly, forgivingly, and savingly relates to human beings in what Buber terms as a dependable, caring, I-*Thou* manner? How, in other words, can one love and worship, put one's whole heart, mind, and will into adoring and serving, an *impersonal* God?

Before taking up this crucial question, however, I want to say a bit more about Tillich's insistence that God cannot be a being among other beings, no matter how transcendently and exaltedly such a God might be imagined or conceived. Tillich offers a discussion of four categories of finite existence by way of clarifying and defending this fundamental claim: *time, space, causality*, and *substance*. According to him, none of these categories can apply to God when God is properly understood as Being-Itself because each category signifies the limitations of finitude.

Then there are what Tillich calls the three ontological elements of finitude: *individuality and participation, dynamics and form*, and *freedom and destiny*. Once again, none of these three can be convincingly and meaningfully applied to God. I will take up first the categories and, second, the elements as Tillich describes them, showing why each of them creates only confusion when applied to God and thus that God cannot rightfully be characterized as a distinct finite being no matter how glorious or majestic such a supposed divine being might be thought to be.

Four Categories of Finitude

The four categories of finitude in Tillich's analysis are time, space, causality, and substance. Since none of these categories applies to God, as Tillich interprets the reality of God, then God cannot properly be understood as one sort of finite being among others. God for Tillich is the source of the courage humans can exhibit in the face of the continuous loss of the past to the present and the continuing confrontation of the fleeting present with an increasingly uncertain future. That future is also bound to end someday—and perhaps at any time—in the death of a particular person. Haunting awareness of death's inevitability fills that person with anxiety, an anxiety that can only be assuaged by the mysterious, pervasive power of God as Being-Itself that grounds, assures, and sustains the temporal being of every finite person. Since God is the ground of being that supports and energizes humans in their perilous finitude, this divine ground cannot itself be a finite being among other finite beings, or even be conceptually analogous to any such beings. It is of an entirely different order of being. For Tillich, God is *no less* than a person but *far more* than that, as the infinite ground of all existent beings.

There is a similar anxiety about space that applies to human lives and that shows the need for experience of the power of Being-Itself (or God) to induce and support sufficient courage for humans to confidently affirm their lives in the face of their desperate need for it and despite their natural anxiety about the uncertainty and uneasiness of procuring and maintaining it. Humans naturally crave a physical space, "the body, a piece of soil, a home, a country, the world." They also need "a social space, a vocation, a sphere of influence, a group, historical period, a place in remembrance and anticipation, a place within a structure of values and meanings. Not to have space is not to be" (1951, 194). But the finitude of humans also means "having no definite place; it means having to lose every place finally" and with that loss, the loss of their own being (1951, 194–95).

This is another indication of the radical insecurity of finitude and of its profound need for the sustaining, motivating, empowering presence of God or Being-Itself. It also shows clearly why God cannot be *a* Being but, in light of the desperate need by all finite beings for the inexhaustible enabling presence of God, must be relied upon and *experienced* as Being-Itself. The finite in all of its forms cries out for and rests upon the infinitude of God, an infinitude experienced firsthand by humans in their everyday lives, and not just thought about or imagined.

The remaining two categories of causality and substance also exhibit their own finitude and need for the counterbalancing presence of the power of Being-Itself, as well as showing clearly and convincingly, for Tillich, why God cannot be rightly and literally regarded as a particular kind of being but must be recognized as Being-Itself. "Causality," he writes, "expresses by implication the inability of anything to rest on itself. Everything is driven beyond itself to its cause," which discloses its insufficiency to sustain itself by itself in its own being—and, thus, its unmistakable finitude (196). Only Being-Itself is free of this fundamental limitation or restriction.

Finally, the category of substance implies one substantial being among others. To be a substance is to be *a* being surrounded and limited by other innumerable substantial beings. All substantial beings are inevitably and incurably finite. And "everything finite is innately anxious that its substance will be lost. This anxiety refers to continuous change as well as to the final loss of substance. Every change reveals the relative nonbeing of that which changes. The changing reality lacks substantiality, the power of being, the resistance against nonbeing" (197). God clearly, at least for Tillich, cannot be a substance, a particular sort of entity, but must be the infinite reality that undergirds and strengthens all finite entities, helping to allay the built-in anxieties of the human ones with sufficient resoluteness and capacity to persist—and even to persist thankfully, responsibly, and creatively—through the temporal span of their finite being.

Three Polar Elements of Finitude

Tillich highlights and distinguishes three polarities of finite existence that do not apply to God but that require the presence and power of God as Being-Itself for their proper coordination and balance in relation to one another. These *polar ontological elements*, as he terms them, are characteristic of all finite beings but do not apply to God. They are participation and individuation, freedom and destiny, and dynamics and form. They are inherently tensional and anxiety producing in finite humans, and the achievement and maintenance of their properly supportive, creative, existential balance is a necessary and constant struggle. This balance is the key to a meaningful human life and, for Tillich, to a richly supportive and sustaining faith in God.

For God, according to Tillich, the polar elements do not and could not exist in and for themselves, a fact that shows once again that God is not and should never be finally conceived as a distinct personal being and that whenever God might be spoken of or portrayed in this fashion, it must always be understood as a symbolical and not literal depiction. God suffuses personal beings with the courage to cope confidently and meaningfully with each of the polar elements but is in no way subject to them or threatened by them. The three ontological elements relate, therefore, only to finite beings and not to God as Being-Itself.

The first of the three elements, participation and individuation, marks the human tendency to neglect or overemphasize the one in favor of the other. Humans crave and hope constantly for maximum realization and recognition of their potential for unique self-realization, on the one hand, but also for being accepted as part of social organizations and groups on the other. Each side of this calculus requires the other, but there is also the constant temptation to maximize the one at the expense of the other. I want to contribute to society and to have my personal worth recognized by society, but I also want to be myself and to develop my own skills, interests, and aspirations to achieve my own distinct selfhood as the gift of my own personal life. I want to be *me* but also to be part of *us*, and there is no formula for achieving the proper balance between the two. God as Being-Itself gives me the motivation, courage, and resolution to devote the years of my life to searching for this balance—a search charged with moral and existential significance for each and every finite person.

The second ontological polarity of elements is the tension between dynamism and form. A stultifying insistence on the adequacy of existing but possibly outlived forms can interfere radically with the need for continuing alertness to the possible need for new ones, for example. Dynamism poses a threat to the long established and familiar, and it is reasonable to be wary of introducing too much of it in ordinary circumstances. But without innovations—timely and sometimes risky innovations in one's personal life, public affairs, or other established practices—there is no adaptation of the old to the new or necessary replacement of the old by the new.

Without cherished traditional ways of thinking and acting, there is no stable context within which innovations can be safely tried and tested. Both are needed at all times, and without them, there would have been no salutary historical revolutions or much-needed personal transformations. But how to keep the two in proper balance with one another in particular contexts can be a serious challenge and the cause of considerable anxiety and uncertainty—both at the personal levels of life and at the levels of communities, institutions, and society. Where can individuals or groups get the courage, vision, and determination to decide how much change to introduce and how much continuity to preserve? Tillich's answer to this question is that in the final analysis such courage is granted and imputed into finite human lives by Being-Itself, the prodding, encouraging, luring power of the ever-present Being-Itself that lies at the heart of their existence as finite and fallible creatures.

Closely related to the first two ontological elements is the third one, the tension between destiny and freedom. My destiny is my "thrownness," to use the philosopher Martin Heidegger's key term—a philosopher who had a profound influence on Tillich's own thinking (Tillich 1951: 196; Heidegger 1996: *passim*). It is what I am given, what I have to work with, in my distinctive nature as a human being bestowed on me at the place, time, and circumstances of my birth. My freedom is what I choose to do with what I have been given in the way of genetic inheritance, family background, social and temporal setting, particular interests and abilities, the outcomes of my former choices as these affect my present challenges and opportunities, and the like.

Tillich points in one place to two extremes in thinking about these matters. One is reading my destiny as a kind of all-controlling, inevitable predetermination or fate; the other is regarding my freedom as absolute and unconstrained by any kind of moral or existential norms. He mentions another existentialist philosopher of his time who stimulated his thought as a philosophical theologian, namely, Jean-Paul Sartre (e.g., Tillich 1951, 201; Sartre 1948). For Sartre, freedom was not bound or directed by any kinds of antecedent norm. Each person has to make up that person's own norms of choice arbitrarily and without any kind of reliable guidance—creating ex nihilo the whole course of the person's life just as an artist creates an artistic production. Human freedom is an *absurd freedom* for Sartre.

But this course of life is fraught with anxiety. Which norms should I choose? How can I create meaning in the context of an absurd and meaningless life? The pole of absolute, unrestricted, unconstrained choice is indistinguishable from absolute meaninglessness and despair. But on the other hand, to try to live someone else's conception of a meaningful life is to sacrifice my liberty to blind conformity, and thus to give up, as far as possible, the distinctiveness of my own destiny: that is, what I am uniquely gifted with as an individual human being. Finding the proper balance between these extremes is an anxious endeavor that never ceases to be such throughout a person's life. For Tillich, God as Being-Itself provides the courage to deal successfully and meaningfully with this lifelong endeavor and the challenges and opportunities it provides for personal growth, maturation, and contribution.

The other pole of freedom and destiny is equally anxiety-ridden and a profound threat to meaningful self-realization. This is the pole of causal determinism, the idea that all of my actions are fixed by causal factors over which I have never had and never will have any personal freedom, choice, or control. I am not a real, self-determining person. I am only a confluence of intersecting, impersonal causes that finally and ultimately constrain and produce the sum total of my thoughts and actions. To my mind, as well as to Tillich's, this idea is thoroughly nihilistic. I am nothing more than a spectator or bystander of actions, none of which is truly my own or the consequences of my own genuinely free decisions.

We are constantly seduced into accepting and believing either side of Tillich's three ontological polarities, but God as Being-Itself gives us the strength and courage to affirm neither at the total expense of the other, and to seek out, successfully conceive, and appropriately implement an ongoing proper balance among them in the trying situations of our ongoing lives. This is an anxious prospect in all of its three aspects, but God enables us to cope with it and act in accordance with it in creative, life-affirming ways. This assurance is the most fundamental part of Tillich's religious outlook and commitment of faith.

The God *Above* God and Yet Meaningfully Available *as* God

Tillich is acutely aware of the paradoxes generated by his ontological conception of God as Being-Itself, on the one hand, and the attitude toward and faith in God as a distinct Person that pervades the biblical religion of the Old and New Testaments, as well as the Jewish and Christian faiths as long and commonly conceived. His ontological God, he proclaims, is "the God above the God of theism" (1952, 187), and yet it is the same God who acts in history, speaks to the prophets, and whose nature as a God of radically transformative, enabling, and forgiving love toward his human creatures is made decisively manifest for Christians in Jesus the Christ.

Here is how he admits to and frankly poses the paradox of the traditional theistic God in its relation to his own ontologically conceived God in one place. Those who accept his ontological account of God as Being-Itself and not as a distinct sort of personal being, he reflects, "are aware of the paradoxical character of every prayer, of speaking to somebody to whom you cannot speak because he is not 'somebody,' of asking somebody of whom you cannot ask anything because he gives or gives not before you ask, of saying 'thou' to somebody who is nearer to the I than the I is to itself." Each such paradox, he continues, "drives the religious consciousness to a God above the God of theism" (1952, 187).

But in doing so, the paradoxes also remind the faithful of the necessary transcendence of all concrete symbols of true faith—including those that routinely portray God as a person—of their pointing beyond themselves to fathomless depths of experience and reality that lie beyond the power of any collection of symbols to adequately describe. God is not "up there" or "out there" somewhere but deep within the day-to-day experience of each human being, and deep within each and every existent thing. God is what enables each existent to persist in its existence and to thrive in ways appropriate to its mode of existence. God transcends persons but is deeply *personal* in the sense of that which gives sustenance, courage, and affirmation of life to each person. The nonpersonal God is profoundly *personal* in this ontological but also everyday and richly experiential sense.

For Tillich, God is the God of the fathomless depths of awareness, of the yawning abyss of mystery that can only be experienced and never literally conceived or described. Beyond all of the words about God, even those of the most articulate and imaginative theologians or philosophers of any given time, there is the mystery and fascination of the *Logos,* of the God whose name cannot be spoken, but whose reality lies beneath and beyond all powers of human description. Just as I can experience an occasion of great joy or terrible grief but can find no way adequately to describe it, so my lips are muted in the presence of the God beyond all capacity of traditional theism to adequately depict or comprehend.

God for Tillich is more like an overwhelmingly formidable presence or power than a distinct person. This conviction enhances rather than diminishes for him the sacred majesty and awesome reality of God, not only from an ontological or philosophical perspective but also in relation to the anxious exigencies and indescribable joys of daily life. Traditional theism and ontology are for Tillich *complements* rather than *adversaries*, each of which has the power to inform and enrich the other in significant fashion. But although each needs the other, they are not equals. The final truth for him resides in the God above God, the God of all the universe and all reality, the proof of whose own reality and absolute existential importance is found finally and most convincingly in the human heart and in the depths of human experience.

Religious Symbols as Revelational Bridges between the Finite and the Infinite

Significant revelational events, experiences, or disclosures are crucial factors in religious traditions, and I called attention to them when discussing the theism of Kierkegaard and Buber. They provide what philosopher of religion William A. Christian refers to as "illuminating suggestions," whose occurrence stimulates further discourse, elaboration, and development within religious communities, some of which may have been brought into existence in the first place by such initial, unforgettable experiences (Christian 1964, 93–112, 245–48). Moses at the burning bush, Jacob wrestling with the angel, Peter's exclamation, "Thou art the Christ, the son of the living God," Paul on the road to Damascus, Muhammad in the cave, Gautama Buddha under the Bodhi Tree—these are familiar examples of such paradigmatic religious discoveries. Each of them led to the development of powerful religious symbols that came to constitute the supporting structures of great religious traditions. The term *suggestions* is the key to understanding the role of such concrete symbolizations in the various forms of religious faith. Religious symbols do not literally describe or portray the fundamental character or constituents of religious communities. They point beyond themselves to indescribable but experienceable realities and truths.

But as Tillich insists, they also somehow *participate* in those realities and truths. The flag as a symbol of one's beloved country is an example he uses that helps to illuminate this point (1957, 42). I see it waving serenely in the breeze, and intense patriotic feelings may be elicited. "This is my believed country, and the flag is its blessed symbol," I think to myself. Now obviously the flag is literally only a swatch of colored cloth, and it has no literal feelings of serenity as it flaps in the wind. But my experience of patriotic fervor is an experience in which the waving flag "participates," in the sense that it is part and parcel of my experience at this time and perhaps of many other times.

In similar fashion, the symbolization of a personal God points beyond itself to an ontological God Tillich calls the power and presence of Being-Itself. The highly symbolic expressions, deeds, utterances, and experiences of the Hebrew Prophets point in the same direction for Tillich, as do the life, teaching, commitment, and agonizing death of Jesus the Christ, as set forth in the Christian New Testament. For Tillich, literalism punctures high-flying symbolic helium-filled balloons, making them deceptive and meaningless. Understanding and responding to them as symbolic expressions sets them free and lets them soar. For him, what lies beneath the symbolisms in each powerful and meaningful religious system, Christian or otherwise, is the universal reality of Being-Itself as the ground of all finite forms of existence.

Critical Discussion of Tillich's View of God

Tillich is entirely right, in my judgment, to insist on the central role of concrete symbols in the expression of all forms of religious faith. But his claim that all such symbols point, in the final analysis, to Being-Itself as the ground of all finite existents, is not as unarguably and universally true as he assumes it to be. He puts a supposedly universal ontology, which he never questions, in place of the various kinds of religious traditions which, as he admits, commend and elicit their own particular kinds of faith.

He does an admirable job of analyzing the various kinds of anxiety that can lurk beneath the awareness of finite human beings, and his existentialist philosophy serves him well in this respect. But his claim that all of these forms of anxiety point to Being-Itself as the ground of being of those who experience such anxieties, while captivating and interesting in its own right, is surely a debatable way of thinking about them. But he uncritically assumes throughout his writings that this way of thinking is universally true and lies behind every kind of religion, including his own radical, non-personalistic reinterpretations of traditional Jewish, Christian, and Muslim theologies' conceptions of God. Implicit in this assumption is a further, unannounced one that seems to take for granted the primacy of an *existential philosophy* to all systems of *religious thought* and their concrete modes of symbolization.

Kierkegaard and Buber, for example, would reject out of hand Tillich's contention that God is ultimately or absolutely impersonal—at least as I interpret their respective theologies in the first chapter of this book. They might even be inclined to regard such a view as blasphemy, a strike at the very heart of their religious faith. For them, it is not an abstract Being-Itself that undergirds all reality, but the living, gloriously, and illimitably *personal* God.

At its best, then, Tillich's philosophical theology shows itself to have the unmistakable air of the parochial, of one highly interesting approach among many to give life and convincingness to a particular religious tradition among others. In saying this, I do not mean to claim that his theology is false, only that its claim to some kind of indisputable final truth is open to serious question. I do want to point out, however, that it would be hard for convinced theists such as Kierkegaard or Buber to find ways of worshipping, serving, and relating to a philosophical abstraction.

Being-Itself is abstract even though Tillich claims it to provide the most powerful and intimate kinds of assurance and support to a person's life. It is not itself a person and consequently has no personality, feelings, motivations, or intentions. Its influence as *love*, if felt or symbolized as such by the individual who is so sustained and guided in the midst of the anxieties inherent in the person's finitude, exists *only in the experience* of the finite individual. Such personal traits as care, love, and concern cannot be attributed to Being-Itself. It is doubtful that this way of thinking would be perceived as an accurate portrayal of their experiences of and references to God by convinced theists. For them, the love of God is experienced in personal relationship with a personal God. Such an I-Thou relationship is the most basic element of Buber's theology, for example.

A second line of critical analysis of Tillichian theology lies in the question of whether or not it is true that every kind of existence must be grounded in some kind of more ultimate principle, power, or pervasive presence beyond itself. Does nature as the multiple orderings of diverse finite entities and their distinctive kinds of relationships require a ground beyond itself? I shall argue later in this book that it does not—scientifically, philosophically, or religiously. In other words, *nature is its own ground.*

For religious naturalism as one significant kind of religious faith, nature requires nothing supernatural or beyond itself that it presupposes or rests on. Nature is the concrete, here-now, accessible, ultimate reality, and it is not dependent on anything else for its continuing existence. Nature is all and everything that there is, has been, or ever will be. For religious naturalism, all real explanations are naturalistic ones. We need not explain nature; we explain whatever admits of explanation in terms of nature.

Is nature, then, a synonym for Being-Itself as Tillich conceives it? It has a similar role, admittedly, but is hardly the same thing. It does not accord with or align with Tillich's special type of ontology that owes a great deal to ancient and medieval reflections on Being and to the phenomenological (e.g., Edmund Husserl) and existentialist (e.g., Martin Heidegger, Jean-Paul Sartre) philosophies that were so influential—and rightly so as correctives to mostly abstract and exclusively conceptual modes of philosophy—in his own century.

Paul Tillich was to my mind the greatest Protestant philosophical theologian of the twentieth century. He was such not so much because of the total convincingness of his thought, two aspects of which I have brought into serious critical consideration in this section, but because it exposes and brings into perspective so many ways of reflecting deeply on the plausibility of theistic religious systems such as those of Judaism, Christianity, and Islam.

Tillich is an extremely thoughtful thinker, and for that, all who reflect on religion and philosophy should be grateful. He raises deep questions that, once raised, demand thoughtful responses. And many of his positive assertions also kindle thoughtful responses on the part of the careful reader. The collection of his sermons called *The Shaking of the Foundations* and first published in 1948, not long after the earth-shaking horrors of the Holocaust, the atomic bombing of Hiroshima and Naga-saki, and the gruesome world war, shows him clearly to have been a man of powerful and exemplary Christian faith. We can be deeply inspired by the earnestness and deep-probing character of his thought even as we might be compelled for various reasons to take issue with some of its aspects, and perhaps even with the deepest of those that draw on a certain kind of philosophy and develop its bearings on a traditional form of theistic religious faith.

Conclusion

In this chapter I have brought into view, interpreted, and discussed the significance of another conception of God and defense of the reality of God. God is generally thought of by theists to be a particular sort of being and one possessed of distinctive personal traits. God is a righteous judge, for example, a personal being who reveals his will and purpose to humankind, a God of boundless love and mercy, a holy, saving, enchanting Thou who invites humans into I-Thou relationships—and the like. When one usually and typically thinks about the meaning of the term *God* and its central place in theistic religions of many different sorts—ancient and contemporary, globally Eastern and Western, Northern and Southern, one envisions, above all else, a majestic, holy, transcendent, and yet also radically immanent, personal being. The infinitude of God is thought to stand in stark contrast with the finitude of all of God's creations, but not to such an extent as to eclipse or eliminate God's eminently personal nature.

As we have seen, however, the renowned theist and Christian theolo-gian Paul Tillich takes strong issue with this conception of God. For him, to conceive of God as an existing person among other existing persons is a grave mistake. This is to make God finite and limited in many ways if it is construed as a *literal* depiction of God. But God as Tillich conceives God is a reality that lies far beyond any sort of limitation, including the limitation of being a distinct being with a distinct kind of personality. This is so for Tillich, no matter how perfect, exalted, sublime, or holy that personality might be conceived to be. God cannot be *a* person, *a* kind of particular existent of any kind, and truly be God.

The nature of God is accurately and existentially understood only when God is recognized as Being-Itself, the inexhaustible power of being that underlies and supports all finite beings. In particular, it is the power, motivation, strength, and presence of persistence and courage that inhabit, direct, and support the life of each and every finite human person and in the face of all existential anxiety that threatens the person's powers of self-affirmation. It does so in the face of the ominous threats of guilt and self-condemnation, emptiness and despair, and fate and death—threats built into the very existence of finite human persons. What plays this essential role in the life of every finite person cannot, for Tillich, be itself a person. It can only be Being-Itself, an impersonal but uniquely enabling force, presence, or power that lies behind and makes possible the continuing existence of finite beings of all sorts, including human persons.

Tillich concedes that God can be appropriately *symbolized* in religious thought, discourse, and ritual as a personal being. But such symbolizations as God the Father, God the Son and incarnate Christ, God the Spirit or constant Inspiration and Comforter, God the Thou who yearns for fellowship and communion with God's human creatures, and the like, must be seen theologically and philosophically by humans as pointing beyond themselves to a reality they have no final power to adequately express or convey.

The symbolic way of characterizing and designating God points to a "God above God," not to a literally personal God. Such symbolism has undeniable great use and significance in theistic religions and, I might add, in polytheistic ones. This is pragmatically so, for Tillich, and he is well aware of this fact as a practicing theologian. But it is ontologically not so, a truth disclosed for Tillich in the depths of experience of every finite human being. Tillich's phenomenological and existential philosophy takes precedence over claims to the personhood of God in traditional theistic religions.

But there is danger in Tillich's theological perspective of destroying what makes theistic religions such powerful sources of inspiration, comfort, and strength—what motivates their passionate concern for social justice, and what most fundamentally informs their reverential, worshipful responses— namely, faith in a loving, caring, forgiving, righteous, just, and personal God. Such a personal God is commonly regarded in theistic religions as the ground of all being, but as a profoundly *personal ground*, not Tillich's more abstract, impersonal Being-Itself.

In a sense, I think he substitutes an *abstract philosophy* for *living religion*, if the latter is to be accurately thought of and described. When Tillich mentions in one of his sermons in *The Shaking of the Foundations* "the living God" of whom the Psalmist of Psalm 90 speaks, and then abruptly in the following paragraph of "the infinite gap between himself [the Psalmist] and God," it is not at all clear how the infinite gap between Being-Itself and ordinary existing beings could be bridged for any existent, allowing for meaningful relationships between Being-Itself and finite human beings (1948, 69).

For him, the philosophy is made less abstract and much more credible when set within the context of finite experience, where the sustaining, motivating, encouraging, enabling power of Being-Itself is experienced by finite persons who find in it respite and courage for their continuing lives in the face of the pervasive anxieties inherent in their finitude. I think he is in touch with something vitally important in this regard, but I fail to be convinced that such experiences cannot be interpreted and assuaged in relation to commitment to a personal God. The testimonies of living theistic religions seem to me to give ample assurance that they can.

And I do not mean by this statement that "God," conceived as a living personal Being is here only symbolically referred to and thought of in the manner Tillich prescribes. I mean that we need to take seriously the possibility that God is personally experienced as Buber, Kierkegaard, and other theists have described. Is it really only Being-Itself, an impersonal reality that they experience? Is a personal God necessarily finite, as Tillich claims?

It would take some doing to persuade traditional theists that this is so, and I do not think that Tillich succeeds in his carefully developed enterprise to accomplish this end. His thought certainly *intrigues*, but I do not think that it universally *compels*, either in principle or in fact. I make these statements, not by way of defending the existence of a personal God but in describing the powerful, life-affirming experience of belief in it for enormous numbers of persons through the ages.

He is well within his rights to defend the idea that God is rightly conceived as Being-Itself, and that the latter is a universal principle, presence, or power lying behind all authentic forms of religious commitment. But the universality of this principle—despite its evident phenomenological and existential appeal—remains in question. Tillich poses a carefully developed possibility for our consideration, and for that we can be grateful. But despite his sagacity in doing so, he sets forth only one way of looking at the question of the character and existence of God, a way that admits of other outlooks and perspectives, including those that deny God's existence, that seek for other ways to interpret religious experience, or seek to set aside religion altogether.

God as Being-Itself is not an undeniable fact of human existence, as Tillich often in his writing leaves the impression of pointing out, insisting, and urging, but one important way of thinking about the nature and significance of the concept of God among many others. In other words, God for many is a *living personal presence*, fully capable of being literally, and not just symbolically, experienced and described as such. This is a different ontology from the one Tillich assumes and advances.

Perhaps the natural sciences of today can help us to mull profitably over these questions, and especially the ones that might relate directly in some manner to the question of the existence of God. I shall turn our attention in the fifth chapter to a reputable scientist who seeks to show how the natural sciences, and especially his own field of quantum physics, can lend itself to offering evidence for, or at least complementary perspective on, the possible existence of God as a personal, living Being. The scientist is the British physicist-theologian John Polkinghorne. His approach to this issue is interestingly different from those of Buber, Kierkegaard, and Tillich, and it offers yet another way to approach the question of the putative nature and reality of God.

Chapter Four

God and History

Paul Tillich was deeply influenced by the thought of *the* German philosopher of the nineteenth century, Friedrich Wilhem Joseph Schelling. This was especially the case with Schelling's conception of God as the absolute *urgrund* (or "nameless abyss") out of which the whole history of the universe and all of its modes of existence—inorganic as well as organic—come into being. At one place in his writing, Schelling speaks of this ground not as a particular kind of being but as the "infinite potence of Being" or "infinite competence of Being-Itself" (2020, 44). What can be known about God is the outcome of God's being known in history, starting with the creation of the world and culminating (but not ceasing) in the humble revelatory incarnation or *kenosis* ("emptying") of God into Jesus the Christ.

But the whole span of history, human or otherwise, after the time of Christ to the present and beyond, should also be seen as the ongoing manifestation of God as the origin and continuing source of all existence and of all existing beings. This manifestation or *revealing*, although continuing through the entire history of the universe, is also a *concealing* because there is no way in which the ultimate ground of all existence can be adequately or literally thought to be some sort of singular existing entity, personal or otherwise.

The "God above God" (to use Tillich's term) is therefore not a distinctive kind of existing being but *Being-Itself*. As such, it is paradoxically, both ground and abyss. To put the matter in Schelling's terms, God is *quod sit* ("that it is") but not a *quid sit* ("what it is"). It is ultimately real but ultimately nameless, in other words. To put the point in Tillichian parlance, its reality can be couched in deeply meaningful and life-sustaining symbolic forms, but it can never be literally depicted or described. Humans can also *experience* intimate *relationship* with God, as Buber contends, even though readily acknowledging the fathomless *mystery* of God. And the pervasive paradoxicality of Kierkegaard's interpretations of the will and purpose of God can be readily understood. A nonparadoxical God or putatively transparent revelation of God in all its respects could lay no claim to adequacy or truth.

The cup (or capacious bowl) of the world into which God's truth is poured is always radically overflowing with what can only be humbly and partially alluded to, never precisely conceived or stated. Buber, Kierkegaard, Tillich, and Schelling all concur on this essential point. Feuerbach, for his part, tends to treat the language of theistic religion far too literally and rationalistically for their taste. Paradox, indirection, or symbolic language for them is by implication, if not to the explicit extent of Tillich's insistence and analysis, the necessary limen or middle area between the extremes of that which is strictly rational, intelligible, and provable on the one hand, and mere nonsensical babble, on the other. It is a delicate balancing act but one on which all profoundly meaningful and avowedly saving religion—theistic or otherwise—crucially depends.

Schelling offers three parallel approaches to understanding the process whereby the Absolute or Unnamable becomes the salvific God of Christian revelation. The first approach is entirely a priori or rational in character, with no reference to anything beyond reason. The second is principally *empirical* in its character and, as such, applicable to the whole of nature and to life on earth, including the lives of human beings. The third approach is exclusively *revelational* or divinely bestowed and therefore also empirical in its own manner. It pertains particularly to the vitally important, desperate need for continuing "courage to be" in human life about which Tillich eloquently and wisely speaks and places at religion's heart (Tillich 1952). In what follows, I will discuss each of these approaches, and then proceed to a critical discussion of Schelling's conception of God and of its crucial role in each of the three approaches.

A Priori Reasoning

Schelling contends that a purely self-contained reason that makes no reference to the experienced world can provide an important clue to the reality of God, although it cannot substitute for the experience throughout history of the gracious, divinely initiated revelations of God. Such reasoning provides a kind of background for or framework within which God's creation of the world and ongoing activity within it can be understood. Schelling talks in this connection of three aspects of such a priori reasoning. These phases flow out of but also back into one another as we continue to think of them. The first phase is one of pure, unlimited, unconditioned possibility.

It passes over into or empties into a phase of a kind of substrate analogous to Aristotle's *prime matter* devoid of qualities of any kind and yet able to give support to such qualities. This second phase is a kind of bare *quod* or "thatness" with no *quiddity* or specific character. Schelling may have in mind here the passage in the biblical book of Genesis that speaks of the earth as being "without form and void" (1:2) prior to its further creation by God. But this substrate also provides a basis for a type of existence with character, namely, an existing, many-splendored world. The marvelous qualities of the latter point back to the possibilities posed by the second stage, and it, in turn, points back to its origin in the unbounded, as-yet-unrealized possibilities of the first stage.

Such reasoning, Schelling contends, gives insight into the absolute, unlimited freedom with which God creates the world, in its three phases of completely unbounded, and then more limited possibility, and finally of more specific and qualitative actuality. But the last phase has its own history of ongoing creativity and possibility that point back to their origin and continuing support from the phase of unlimited possibility and unqualified freedom from which they have arisen and by which they are sustained (Schelling 2020, 41–56).

Even though this process of a priori reasoning is for Schelling non-referential and entirely self-contained, it evokes images of the world of experience and of the grounding of this world in the boundless creativity and unlimited support of God. God, in turn, can be recognized, not as some kind of existing being among other distinctive beings but as the source and ground of all particular kinds of existence. Here we can see at least a partial basis and inspiration for Tillich's contention that God cannot be said to "exist" but only to be conceived as "Being-Itself."

Ordinary Empirical Revelatory Evidence

For Schelling, revelation is *empirical* in two senses of the term. The first of these is experience of the history of the world and of both everyday and markedly enchanting or sublime experiences of particular aspects of the world. The second is the special religious experiences of great religious leaders that, when handed down in sacred scriptures or by other means, can serve as experienceable inspirations, revelations, and teachings for the members of a religious community regarding ultimate religious truth.

I refer to the first here as "ordinary empirical evidence," even though it can also convey important religious meaning in the form, for example, of natural theology or of profound experiences of the sanctity of nature. The words of the nineteenth Psalm in the Hebrew Bible are an excellent example:

> The heavens are telling the glory of God; and the firmament
> proclaims his handiwork.
> Day to day pours forth speech, and night to night declares
> knowledge.
> There is no speech, nor are there words; their voice is not heard.
> Yet their voice goes out through all the earth, and their words
> to the end of the world (Psalm 19: 1–4).

In other words, the reality of God is made evident by the *works* of God throughout the whole of nature when it is recognized and revered as God's creation. This is the third, qualitative or *quid* (possessed of attributes) and not just the second or *quod* (merely existent, featureless, devoid of any specific attributes, merely substrate, world), deduced as phases in the world's origin and development by Schelling's a priori analysis. The heavens and the earth declare the glory of God with every passing day, but they do so with the more general and not the more specific form of extraordinary revelatory experiences to be next referred to as aspects of Schelling's thinking about God. The vehicle of revelation in this instance is not nature or the history of nonhuman nature but the history of the revelatory experiences of especially perceptive, receptive, and saintly humans throughout human history—humans responsive not only to the sacred voices of God resounding throughout nature but to the assumedly more direct, awesome, compelling voice of God in special, divinely initiated encounters with God.

Let us consider Schelling's discussion of this second kind of revelation, which for him constitutes the principal source and basis of the Christian view of God. In contrast with Schelling's a priori derivation of God's reality, this manifestation is for him empirical, as are the revelations of God in countless aspects of the cosmos or divinely created nature.

Extraordinary Empirical Revelatory Evidence

In Schelling's interpretation of Christian revelation, there are seven stages whereby the pure potency or unbounded possibility of God becomes various kinds of actuality. The first stage is the transformation of this possibility into the actuality of the substrate, the basis on which a universe with qualities or forms can be created. Since the substrate is a divine creation, Schelling is evidently opposed to the idea that God creates the world ex nihilo or "out of nothing." God creates the substrate devoid of character first, and then the qualitative universe out of the substrate, as two passings from God's first phase of pure possibility to the emergence of two new kinds of actuality.

Thus, God creates the qualitative world by converting it out of the possibilities posed by the substrate. In the meantime, God's pure possibility is allowed to pass over into God's only begotten son, Jesus the Christ, which constitutes a fourth kind of divine action recounted in Christian revelation. The fifth kind of creative activity to which Schelling points is the passing over of the possibilities posed by both God as the Father of Christ and of Christ himself as their jointly created Holy Spirit. All three are then the one true God, and God is seen as personal in each of God's three aspects.

The divine personality is enhanced by the creation of humans as persons—persons with whom God can enter into personal relationships. Schelling sees human beings as the crown and culmination of the earth's creation by God. There is no suggestion of their biological *evolution*; Charles Darwin and Alfred Russel Wallace were as yet unheard of in the first half of the nineteenth century. The seventh stage of the whole creative and revelatory process for Schelling, as for most Christians, is the incarnation or *kenosis* of God—or more accurately, the Son of God—into the human being, Jesus of Nazareth. Jesus is then depicted by later Christian thought as both fully human and fully divine, God's most exemplary, normative, binding revelation of God's will, purpose, and nature to God's human creatures.

In Jesus, God offers God's saving love to all of God's human creatures and God's humble willingness to suffer as they suffer, offering God's saving presence and power in the midst of their suffering. God becomes finite, in other words, to identify with and support God's finite human creatures in the face of all of the perils, disappointments, setbacks, and uncertainties of their finitude. In this way, God is able also to identify intimately and personally with their accomplishments, satisfactions, aspirations, hopes, and joys.

God's becoming a personal being after first being conceived as the absolute, namely, as yet unmanifested and unexercised freedom of pure possibility, is consistent with Tillich's contention that God as Being-Itself is ultimately impersonal. Schelling's account of the main content of Christian revelation, and of the *experiential* recognition and appropriation of that revelation into human life, follows close upon his earlier a priori description of God and of God's creation of the world. But his insistence on special revelation as primarily *experiential* in its function and form is extremely important. Revelation, as Kierkegaard insisted, is the transformation of life when properly understood. It is far more than just a set of doctrines, beliefs, or conceptual truths. These are aspects of revelation, certainly, but they are more the means to a lifetime's experiences of saving relationships with God, relationships Buber rightly regards as personal, "I-Thou" experiences of the reality of God, for those who put their trust in God (Schelling 2020, 164–85).

Critical Discussion of Schelling's Conception of God

I want now to offer some critical comments about both Schelling's a priori philosophy of religion and his empirical philosophy of assumed experiences of divine revelation set within a Christian framework. I will address the following topics in doing so. The passage from possibility to actuality; the question of by what or whom the purported revelations are ultimately given; the idea of the Father "begetting" the Son (Jesus the Christ); the concept of Father rather than Father-Mother, and of Son rather than Son-Daughter, or some kind of sexless conception; the idea of the Trinity as One in Three, or its intelligibility as an alleged monotheism; the issue of Modalism's or Sabellianism's interpretation of the divine Trinity; the role of symbolic discourse versus literal discourse, for example, that of God's really becoming finite, being tempted, suffering, and dying, in distinction from God's continuing empathetic engagements with humans in their lives without having to become a human being; Tillich's reliance on Schelling but also certain of his improvements over Schelling's thought; questions about the nature of the monotheistic God that remain; and, finally, the status of humans within or in relation to the whole of nature. Many of these critical comments will relate to Christianity as it is commonly portrayed, while some relate more specifically to Schelling's interpretation of the Christian tradition.

I do not understand how a putative pure possibility, devoid of any specific character or traits, could create or give rise to anything, much less a whole, multifaceted and multifeatured universe. For me, all creation requires some existing thing out of which, on the basis of which, or by the agency of which other things are made or brought into being. In other words, all creation is transformation of or by means of something already existing. An existent God can be conceived as the creator of the universe, but a not-yet, *merely possible* God cannot logically be so conceived. Tillich's interpretation of God as ultimately Being-Itself poses a similar problem, but at least it is the idea of *Being-Itself* as opposed to Schelling's idea of God as ultimately *Possibility-Itself.*

This problem poses the further problem of by what or whom the ordinary revelations of the natural world are produced, and the further problem of by what or whose ultimate agency the special revelations claimed by the Christian faith are brought into being. In Schelling's account, both of these kinds of revelation have their ultimate source in pure, boundless, characterless possibility, not in God as a personal, loving being. God is only derivatively the latter, not primordially or purposively so. The revelations putatively brought to light by usual Christian faith are ultimately God's self-disclosures, not those of a selfless pure possibility.

In other words, a possibility requires a ground of its being. Sheer possibility cannot serve as the featureless ground of anything. The philosopher Alfred North Whitehead had the good sense to ground so-called pure possibility in the primordial nature of God and in this way to denote its grounding in an actuality—assuming that we take into account his depiction of God's full reality as the interweaving of God's primordial nature with God's consequent nature or God's necessary relations with a coeval, always existing, world (Whitehead 1975, 65–66). Whatever one may think about Whitehead's conception of God or about his theoretical metaphysics as a whole, at least he had the good sense to recognize that even so-called *pure possibility* requires a real metaphysical basis or ground, in contrast with the cart-before-the-horse approach of Schelling, which has actuality resulting from groundless, pure, ultimate possibility. I will have a bit more to say about Whitehead's metaphysical interpretations of the role of God, as he conceives of God, after my critical analysis of Schelling's interpretations of the nature of God.

The idea of the Father "begetting" or giving birth to the Son is also obscure, as is Schelling's idea that God becomes a person only with, or in contrast with, the birth of the Son as a person. Equally obscure is the idea of the two together bringing into existence a third "person or personality" of the Holy Spirit (2020, 171–72). Is God only derivatively rather than primordially three? If so, what is the source of all three? Is it an impersonal possibility-itself? And is this idea intelligible? Schelling's account also makes it sound as if the Father somehow sires the Son, and then that the two together somehow create the Spirit, perhaps by some kind of timeless outflowing or mystical emanation.

Furthermore, the question is raised of why God must be conceived as Father rather than Father-Mother, and the Son as just that, rather than as Son-Daughter. Why, more fundamentally, must God be conceived as a sexual being in the first place? Would not some sort of sexually neutral language be more appropriate? Schelling seems to be oblivious to this problem, itself evidence of the *patriarchal age* in which the doctrine of the Trinity was first formulated and promulgated.

Then there is the problem of how the three "persons" of the Trinity can also be conceived as the manifestations of the one true God. In other words, how can trinitarianism be said to be a form of monotheism? Schelling's answer to this question is presumedly that Son and Spirit emanate from the Father, and that all three emanate from the single principle of the pure possibility from which everything else flows, including the natural world. But this answer only poses the question again of how pure possibility can produce any kind of actuality.

Sabellianism or Modalism is a traditionally unorthodox or heretical answer to this question in the history of Christianity, but Schelling's answer to it as a kind of emanation from Father to Son, and then to Spirit, is a different sort of explanation. The modalist explanation, officially rejected by the early Church, is that the Trinity is nothing more nor less than the three ways God has revealed Godself to the world—a Trinity of modes of *revelation* rather than of divine *essence*. This answer is more intelligible than Schelling's answer, but it is not consistent with the emanational view he propounds, an emanation that puzzlingly and unconvincingly originates in so-called *pure* but yet somehow also *active* or *activating* possibility.

A whole area of thought and interpretation that is fundamental in Tillich's monotheistic and yet Trinitarian theology is Tillich's insistence on the symbolic rather than literal character of language about God. For Tillich as for Schelling, behind all that can be said about God, God's creation of the world, the Trinity, the Incarnation, and so on, is a vast area of abysmal mystery—so much so that, for Tillich, we need recourse to symbolical rather than literal statements, doctrines, and practices. These can only feebly point to what they may endeavor to express. All putative revelations to humans of the nature of God, of the ways of God, and of God's creative activities, while deeply meaningful, must not be confused with literal depictions or expressions. God for us, and God in Godself are two different—and yet not totally different—things. Schelling also believes this to be the case, of course, but Tillich's recourse to symbol, myth, and story instead of literal depiction is to my mind a better way of getting at it than Schelling's way.

Another area of questioning with reference to Schelling's interpretation of the Christian account of divine revelation is that of the high God's emptying into the human being Jesus, the Jesus who refers to God as his Father, relies upon the Father day-by-day, and prays to God constantly as if he were one of God's creatures. If the trinity is an enigmatic approach to the nature of the God of revelation, the incarnation is even more mysterious and conceptually confounding. Is *all* of the Son present in the Jesus of the first century CE, for example, or only a part? Does God pray to Godself in the person of Jesus or only *seem* to do so? Can God incarnated as the man Jesus really be susceptible to serious temptations as other finite humans are? Can God literally experience the bitter anguish and at least temporary despair of the cross?

On this last question, consider Buber's interpretation of the history of God's revelations to the Jewish people, as recorded in the Hebrew Bible. Buber's God yearns for intimate relations with God's human creatures. This view of God sees God as a God of profound empathy with the plight of sinful humanity but not as any literal sense incarnate in a human being. God remains God and could not conceivably have become a man. Becoming a man is in no sense necessary for a satisfying revelation and experience of God's loving, forgiving, saving relationships with God's human creatures. There is no place in Judaism for the idea of the suffering of the God-Man Jesus on the cross as some kind of sacrificial atonement and satisfaction of God's judgment for the sinfulness of fallen humanity. Not only does the idea of the incarnation unnecessarily blur the distinction between human beings and God, it is for both Jews and Muslims a kind of blasphemy or dangerous confusion of the infinite and the finite, the absolute and the limited. Why, then, is it so important for Christians and the Christian conception of revelation? Tillich has a ready answer to this question, while Schelling does not.

Tillich's answer is that the idea of the incarnation of God in Jesus the Christ is a powerful and transformative symbolization of God's empathetic, merciful, saving love for God's human creatures, a divine willingness to enter into, experience, and share at firsthand and in great depth the threats, failures, and anxieties of finite human existence—and to raise humans thereby to a new level of saving trust and transformation. This account is not for Tillich *just* a symbol or myth. It is *everything* that a symbol or myth can be and that a mere literal depiction could not be.

This idea too I regard as an improvement, not only of what seems to me to be Schelling's more literal interpretation of this part of the standard Christian conception of divine revelation, but also of the forcefulness and effectiveness of the story of Jesus's life, ministry, and agonizing death in the first century of our era. The accompanying story of his triumphant resurrection symbolizes the newness of life God mercifully and lovingly offers to all of God's human creatures, not just in some possible life to come after death but where it is already desperately needed: in the here and now.

The next part of Schelling's interpretation of God and the work of God, as set forth in the Christian account of divine revelation that I want to make critical mention of here, is the status Schelling gives more or less unquestioningly to human beings on earth. He sees humans as the crown of creation and the apex of all life on earth rather than as an important but also humble participant of the earthwide community of all of its life forms. There is no suggestion of their long evolution in billions of years of life on earth, no inclusion in this history of the autonomy of an earth made capable by divine impetus and guidance of gradually and eventually producing the emergence of the human species. In other words, humans are seen as separate from the earth and not as an intimate part of its innate physical and natural processes. The earth, in consequence, is not seen as their home. They are aliens whose home is elsewhere, a destination to be hoped for and striven for throughout the mortal life of humans here on earth.

There is thus a kind of denigration of the earth in Schelling's assumption about the status of humans, a denigration that sees the earth for humans, and *only for humans* out of all of the billions of life forms on earth in the present and from the past, as a mere launching pad toward, or temporary period of trial for, a far better life to come. If humans are not extremely thoughtful and careful, this view of things can turn out to have disastrous consequences for the future of the earth and its life forms—including our own—in our time. As the global climate crisis of today's world is making increasingly apparent, human technology, habitat usurpation, and arrogant and unjust misuse of the earth's features is radically endangering the whole earth and all of its creatures, human and nonhuman alike. Our principal focus needs to be *here* and not in some imagined life to come. God is with us here, if at all, and God's empathy, if there is a God, presumedly extends generously and fully to every aspect of the earth, not just to human beings.

Finally, even though Schelling lived in a time that had only recently discovered that the earth is not the center of the universe, he could not have been aware in his time that this supposed focus or center is only one tiny part of an enormous galaxy, and that this enormous galaxy is only one of billions of such galaxies throughout an incredibly far-flung universe. His basically earth-centered universe of divine revelation, even though a product of the sophisticated thought processes of his undoubted genius, is sadly cramped and outmoded by present-day scientific standards.

The lesson I draw from this fact is that, if there is such a thing as natural theology, it is never finished but always unfolding and demanding fresh interpretation and understanding throughout history. And if there is a God, this God must be active throughout history—past, present, and future—and visions of God must be constantly adapted to the requirements of changing times. Schelling's conception of God, for all of its fascinating depth, lacks in important ways the dimension of adequate breadth, as seen from the perspective of our own century. And who knows how it will fare in yet more distant times?

A Bit More on Whitehead's Metaphysical God

Since I mentioned above the need for a metaphysical status of possibility, as opposed to Schelling's tendency to see it as original, groundless, and free-floating, I want to offer in this section a brief account of the important place of God in Whitehead's metaphysics. I applaud Whitehead for his seeing the need for a metaphysical status for the realm of possibility and not for just taking it for granted as metaphysicians are sometimes, if not often, wont to do. The fact that this status is *in God* for Whitehead is relevant for this book's inquiries into various conceptions of God in the history of religion and the history of philosophy. It is especially relevant in view of the fact that Whitehead takes Christian revelation implicitly into account in his descriptions of the nature of God.

Whitehead discusses two kinds of possibility in his metaphysics: *pure* possibility and *real* possibility. *Both are grounded in actuality.* The ordered realm of *pure* possibilities of all kinds is grounded in the primordial nature of God, and the *real* possibilities are resident in all of the already accomplished facts of an ever-evolving reality and series of epochal worlds or cosmic epochs. It is especially important to note that, for Whitehead, God *needs* the world every bit as much as the world needs God. This is because God has a timeless, primordial nature in which the whole range and order of pure possibilities are envisioned. These exist in God whether they are ingressed or incorporated into aspects of the ongoing world or not. When they become ingressed into some aspect of experienceable or conceivable reality, they can then become real possibilities posed by that reality. For example, swim bladders came into existence at some point of the past in our cosmic epoch, and, with their emergence, real possibilities of further evolutionary development for fish were brought into view (Kauffman 2008, 132). But the pure possibilities, capable of becoming realizable and real, already existed in the primordial nature of Whitehead's God. Humans can imagine some new possibilities suggested by old actualities, but God is capable—by Whitehead's reckoning—of imagining *all* possibilities. This may be hard to conceive, but it at least it gives possibility a status in some kind of actuality.

I should also note in passing that a first-class, highly creative mathematician of Whitehead's undoubtful caliber might have found it easier than most of us to conceive of mathematics as exploration of possibilities that would be less imaginable or discoverable in less lofty mathematical modes of thought. The expert mathematician can be strongly tempted to think that the mathematical discoveries and imaginative conceptions that turn out to have great heuristic and hypothetical value in interpreting empirical phenomena were somehow "out there" awaiting discovery all along.

Most markedly, the experiences of God as a living person require God's intimate involvement in the affairs of the world. This enables God to be fully aware of the real or realized possibilities posed by every evolving stage of the past actual world. This involvement, when woven against the background of the pure possibilities of God's primordial nature, does three things for Whitehead. It enables God to be a conscious person in full touch with the world, and it enables God to be judge and lure toward what is best for each and every phase of new development in the world. Furthermore, it enables God to be consciously aware, with profound empathy, of the sufferings of the world, and particularly of its human forms of life. Whitehead therefore famously describes God as "the great companion, the fellow sufferer who understands" (1975, 351). There is a deep sense, therefore, in which Whitehead's God is *always incarnate* in or intimately related with the affairs of the world, a continual, everlasting incarnation that persists through all cosmic epochs. Whitehead's God also preserves forever in *his* memory all of the attained goods of the past actual world (the traditional sexism in thinking about God persists).

I am particularly interested here in showing how Whitehead locates possibility in actuality, giving it a metaphysical status in one of the two natures of God as well as in God's continual involvements with the affairs of the world. This development of the concept of God also enables God to take fully into account the possibilities already realized in the processes and affairs of the past actual world. In contrast with Schelling's view of possibility, it is nowhere and nowhen present *by itself*. Its root is always in something (or somethings) already existent. And its ultimate locus is not only in the past actual world but in the primordial nature of God.

In either event, possibility, pure or real, is already somewhere, and it is never primordial or having some sort of reality in and by itself, as it seems to have for Schelling. I say all of this, not because I endorse Whitehead's concept of God. I do not, and I agree with my friend George Allan, who has written a recent book (Allan 2020) in which he convincingly defends a version of Whitehead's metaphysics in which there is no God and no necessary role for God. Whitehead's thought has fascinated both of us for many years, but it has not persuaded us to become convinced Whiteheadian monotheists.

Whitehead's possibly mathematically inspired, Platonist conception of *pure* possibility is for me unconvincing, and this criticism applies to Schelling as well. All newness of any kind is transformation of some kind of oldness. From whence did it all originate, then? My answer is that there is no origination of the world, nature, or the cosmos out of nothing or by some kind of ultimate, nonnatural agency. I anticipate here my sustained critique of theism later in this book, but I do so here by way of criticizing the idea of *pure*, as opposed to *real*, possibility, and therewith also of the need for God as the repository or envisagement of the whole order of supposed pure possibilities. For me, all possibility has its seat, origin, or derivation in and out of past, already existing, actualities.

For example, the invention of the wheel as a new kind of real possibility, now actualized, may have been suggested early on by the rolling of logs, then of a segment of a log, and then of connecting two such segments by some sort of axle. A boiling tea kettle may have suggested the power of steam to do work. The flight of birds suggested to the Wright Brothers essential principles of controlled human flight. The parabolic path of a thrown object on earth can suggest both the elliptical paths of the planets and the influence of gravity on all material bodies. And so on. In other words, all new possibilities have their basis in already realized older actualities.

"Why does something (e.g., the universe) exist rather than nothing?" is a spurious question that need not imply the existence of God, in my view. There has always been, and there will always be, something or somethings out of which new things can arise, and this point applies to the whole range of possibilities as well. In the metaphysics I personally favor and endorse, two things are primordial and have always existed in some shape or form: *matter-energy* and *time*.[1] Both are without beginning or ending, and both, as well as the creative processes the two of them in conjunction make possible, produce all actuality through endless time and all of the new possibilities of origination and development posed by these two actualities. Hence, there is no such thing as Schelling's absolute possibility devoid of all character and no need for Whitehead's primordial nature of God as the locus of all so-called pure possibilities.

Surely Whitehead's God is intelligent enough to imagine, solely on the basis of his consequent nature or ongoing experiences of the everlasting past actual world, new possibilities for ingression into the processes of an ongoing, never-ending world. And Schelling's idea of the universe's arising out of some kind of pure possibility would no longer be required. Some sort of existing universe has always been and always will be, in my view (and also in Whitehead's). God could still be conceived as an essential part of this universe—an immanent God rather than a radically transcendent God of the sort imagined by Schelling—but there is no need for his God conceived, ultimately, as some sort of pure, unbounded, featureless possibility.

My final critical comment applies to Tillich as well as to Schelling. To refer to God as either Being-Itself (Tillich) or as Pure Possibility (Schelling) leaves unresolved the question of whether or not God is truly and ultimately personal. If not, then most of traditional theism, which speaks constantly of God in a personal manner, goes out the window. The same is true of its conception of divine revelation. One might as well speak, symbolically or not, of God as being ultimately *nature*, which would make Christianity and Judaism, to say nothing of Islam, versions of religious naturalism or ultimately indistinguishable from it.

It is one thing to speak of the tension between what is *revealed* of God and what must always be *concealed* from the understanding of finite beings such as ourselves. But it is another to lay such heavy stress as Schelling and Tillich do on our inability to have anything like a clear conceptual understanding of God as to render the very idea of God radically opaque and unsure. God is either ultimately personal or not. To mince words on this issue is to strike at the heart of theism as traditionally conceived.

Conclusion

I have continued in this fourth chapter to lay out an exploratory path of investigation into the question of whether a convincing case can be made for the existence and nature of a monotheistic God. In doing so, I have drawn primarily on aspects of the thought of Schelling here but also alluded, where it seemed to me important, to aspects of the thought of Paul Tillich and Alfred North Whitehead. Three aspects of Schelling's musings on God were brought into view: his a priori proof of the ontological necessity of God's pure possibility as the source of all forms of existence—including God's existence as a distinctive personal being;

his appeal to the ample evidences of God he perceives in the history of the natural world; and his reliance on the history of revelation or divine self-disclosure, as recorded principally in the Christian scriptures that include both the Hebrew Bible (or *Tanakh*) and the Greek New Testament.

The first stage makes no explicit reference to experience of any kind, while the second and third make reference to experiences by human beings of the pervasive mystery, wonder, and sacredness of their world, seen as evidential pointers to the reality of God, and then to outstanding, formative experiences of God's nature and ever-present relationship, judgment, help, and power testified to by the religious geniuses or awesomely perceptive and inspired spokespersons for God of the past. These latter are most markedly the Christian ones for those of Christian persuasion. Contained within the unfolding history of divine revelation, as Schelling analyzes it, is the person of God the Father, his giving birth to his Son Jesus the Christ, and their joint emanation of the Holy Spirit.

The resultant character of God is that of a triune person or a three-person, and yet, entirely monotheistic, God. God's kenosis or incarnation on earth in the human being Jesus whose agony on the cross provides the most definitive revelation of God's true nature as the humble, empathetic, long-suffering God of limitless love for all of his human creatures. The resurrection of Jesus from the dead testifies to the limitless power of divine goodness over all the forces of evil at work in the world. Schelling is right in seeing this idea as lying at the heart of the Christian tradition, and it has important influence on Whitehead's conception of God, as I indicate in this chapter.

I mount some criticisms of Schelling, Tillich, and Whitehead in this chapter, most notably those dealing with the status of possibility as a problem in metaphysics. I argue that all possibility has its basis in some kind of actuality. Hence, if God exists, God is primordially actual and not derivative from some kind of ultimate pure possibility. This criticism applies particularly to Schelling, but it also has bearing on Tillich's conception of God—or the "God beyond God"—of Tillich's theology. I take issue, however, with Whitehead's contention that the primordial nature of God is required to give status to the ordered realm of all so-called pure possibility.

I argue that there is no such thing as pure possibility. All realizable or real possibility is instantiated in the past actual world (or, more properly, past actual *worlds*) as potential new possibilities implicit in that world or those worlds. New possibilities are posed, therefore, by the past and do not exist in some other timeless metaphysical realm. Here I take issue, not only with Whitehead, but also with Plato. But the main point I wish to make is that if God exists, God exists as an actuality—not as either the outcome of some kind of primordial possibility, nor as some kind of abstract, ill-defined possibility that, in Schelling's telling, becomes a personal being.

Chapter Five

Natural Science and Theological Metaphysics

The natural sciences and religious thought are sometimes, if not generally, thought to be opposed to one another, so that if a person is convinced of the truths of the first, that person cannot logically be committed to the supposed truths of the second. The methods, assumptions, focuses, traditions, and expectations of the two are considered to be so different that they stand in radical opposition to one another—an opposition that permits no conceivable reconciliation as long as the distinct character of each is kept firmly in mind.

A case in point is the evolutionary biologist Richard Dawkins, justifiably acclaimed for his expertise and accomplishment in his particular field of scientific investigation. Speaking of the eighteenth-century Scottish philosopher David Hume's work, *Dialogues Concerning Natural Religion*, Dawkins comments: "What Hume did was to criticize the logic of using apparent design in nature as *positive* evidence for the existence of God. He did not offer any *alternative* explanation for apparent design, but left the question open" (1987, 6).

Dawkins argues that Hume was right to do so and proclaims that Charles Darwin gave us the correct answer, in the mid-nineteenth century, to Hume's open question that was left hanging in the previous century: "Natural selection, the blind, unconscious, automatic process which Darwin discovered, and which we now know is the explanation for the existence and apparent purposeful form of all life, has no purpose in mind. It has no mind and no mind's eye. It does not plan for the future. It has no vision, no foresight, no sight at all. If it can be said to play the role of watchmaker in nature, it is the *blind* watchmaker" (1987, 5). The blind watchmaker of all natural processes, not just those of evolutionary biology, replaces and renders irrelevant, for Dawkins, any need for appeal to God as the creator, sustainer, and purpose-bestower of the universe as a whole or of any of the processes of nature. For him, science and theism are adamantly opposed to one another. In his own field of evolutionary biology, the "blind watchmaker" of immanent natural processes in nature makes unnecessary any need for appeal to the work of a personal deity. Commitment to the assumptions, methods, and procedures of the first renders any appeal to the second as outmoded and superfluous. Religion is necessarily overshadowed, eclipsed, and rendered obsolete by natural science.

I want us to bring Dawkins's view, and that of others who agree with his way of thinking about the relations of natural science and religion, under critical examination in this chapter. I shall do so primarily by discussing the alternative view of another natural scientist, in this case from the field of physics—and especially quantum physics as his own particular field of expertise—the British scientist who later in his life was also ordained as an Anglican priest, John Polkinghorne.

He not only takes strong issue with Dawkins's rejection of theism but also vigorously defends theism in a number of books and does so largely on the basis of what he takes to be the *theological implications of natural science* as he conceives it—and particularly on the basis of his own involvements in and important contributions to the field of quantum physics. I embark on this task not so much in the spirit of personally defending monotheism but in the spirit of complementing my exposition of the defenses of it by Kierkegaard, Buber, Tillich, and Schelling with the defense of it mounted by another one of its eminent, thoughtful, and eloquent defenders. In defending theism, Polkinghorne draws heavily on his experience and expertise as a physicist. By doing so, he also lays special emphasis on what he calls *theological metaphysics* as a comprehensive worldview in which can be placed the important work of natural scientists—hence, the title of the present chapter.

Polkinghorne was a lifetime Christian who died in 2001. His work as a theoretical physicist and his significant contributions to quantum physics, along with those of many others in this field, served only to strengthen his faith in God and not in any way to weaken it: so much so that when he retired from his work as a physicist, he underwent training as an Anglican priest and was ordained as such in 1977. After that time, he worked as priest and theologian, devoting himself to showing what he regarded as the crucial contributions of the natural sciences, when they are properly interpreted and understood, to faith in God.

In the two of his many books to be considered here (1998 and 2000) he portrays metaphysics, that is, his vision of general, all-encompassing reality, as being rooted in and dependent upon the existence and purposes of one personal deity, and this theological metaphysics, for its part, as encompassing and suffusing all other aspects of human life and endeavor. These other aspects include philosophy, art, morality, history, secular culture, daily life and experience, *and the whole of natural science* as a particular field of thought and endeavor. His conception of God is that of a convinced, liberal, Anglican Christian.

We can begin our investigation of Polkinghorne's commitment to belief in God, and of the intimate connections he found this commitment to have with his work as a scientist, by discussing his view of theology as a kind of metaphysics. The theology he most particularly has in mind, of course, is that of Christianity as he interprets its character and significance. We can then investigate, in turn, the following topics of discussion: God conceived as a personal being; the rootage of theological metaphysics in divine revelation; relations of natural science to theological metaphysics; *particular* revelations and the ideal of *universal* truth; and, finally, the cosmological anthropic principle suggested by current physics. This principle is interestingly different from the idea of God as an anthropomorphic *projection* that we saw to be articulated and defended by Feuerbach.

Theological Metaphysics

Polkinghorne regards theology as an *integrating* discipline that brings all of the other major types of inquiry under a common umbrella or "a deeper and more comprehensive matrix of understanding." He has especially in mind such areas of experience and thought as science, aesthetics, morality, and religion—the latter because "first-order investigation of religious phenomena" is part of the task of theology. Theology for him, therefore, "aims to be a true 'theory of everything,' based on the fundamental premise that the Mind and Will of a divine Agent lie behind the multi-level character of our encounter with reality" (2000, 27–28). Thus, while all other specific aspects of experience, life, and the world are partial and encompassed, theology, as Polkinghorne envisions it, is all-encompassing in its task and intent. Its purview is not just religion in the narrower senses of that word but the whole of experienced reality in each of its major dimensions.

Theology is thus a necessary complement to the natural sciences, not opposed to them in practice or principle. Its concern is with the whole of life, and with what gives ultimate meaning and value to life, including the lives of scientists, artists, moral exemplars, philosophers, and all of those who are profoundly impressed with the mystery and wonder of the natural world. The scientists' fascination with and dependence on the elegance and beauty of mathematically framed great theories, their sense of wonder at the inexhaustible depth and complexity of nature, their patient hope for deeper understanding of beguiling natural processes, and their necessary trust in the moral integrity of their fellow scientific workers: all of these outlooks, experiences, and dependencies testify to depths of experience to which theology makes explicit reference and for which it offers the most profound kind of explanation (2000, 16–20). This theological form of explanation is rooted for Polkinghorne in the creation of the world by and its continual reliance on the saving presence, power, and love of God. Faith in God is for him the ultimate making sense of our lives in the world as finite beings. All of the other kinds of intelligibility and trust stem from it and point back to it. In his judgment, this faith is what qualifies theology to be the most adequate kind of metaphysics.

God as a Personal Being

God is certainly the *ground of being* for Polkinghorne, to borrow Tillich's potent phrase. But in contrast to Tillich's thinking, God is literally (and not only symbolically) *a distinct personal being*. The nature of God certainly far exceeds our complete understanding, but God's character as preeminently *personal* is never questioned by Polkinghorne.

God grounds our existential hope for the ultimate triumph of goodness over evil in the world and for sustaining personal courage in the face of the threats to confident self-affirmation in our finite lives, including the inevitability of our approaching deaths, as Tillich also insists (Polkinghorne 1998, 128; 2000, 20–23). But God does so for Polkinghorne as an *existent divine person*—in keeping with the theological convictions of Kierkegaard and Buber and in sharp contrast with the views of Feuerbach and Dawkins.

The distinct divine personhood, which Polkinghorne constantly assumes, explicitly endorses, and ardently defends, also distinguishes his version of theology in a fundamental respect from that of Tillich. God is not only the ground of being for Polkinghorne—and God is assuredly that—*but is also a particular kind of existent being*. This conviction lies at the heart of Polkinghorne's theological metaphysics. God has purposively and personally created the world, continues to sustain it, and is actively involved in its affairs.

Most importantly, as Buber also insists, God has chosen, and faithfully continues to choose, to be in constant saving, self-revealing *relationships* with God's human creatures on planet earth. Science, philosophy, art, morality, politics, day-to-day life, and the history of the world as a whole and of human civilizations on earth turn for Polkinghorne on this central idea, as does his own theological metaphysics. For him, as a convinced Christian, this idea of God's continual loving relationship with God's human creatures is most profoundly and particularly shown by the incarnation of God in Jesus the Christ. In this divine self-emptying or kenosis, "It seems that God is willing to share with creatures, to be vulnerable to creatures, to an extent not anticipated in classical theology's picture of the God who, through primary causality, is always in total control" (1998, 126).

The life, teachings, ministry, and experiences of Jesus, as described in the four Gospels, *also constitute for Tillich*, as himself a Christian theologian, the most definitive, inspiring, and revelatory *symbolic* depictions of the nature of God as Being-Itself. Being-Itself is brought to its most vivid and compelling manifestation in Jesus the Christ who exemplifies the gracious reality of its constant presence and saving power for the world and for every aspect of finite human life (Tillich 1951, 135–37). The depths of evil require for their subjugation far greater depths of goodness, and those depths of goodness, represented for Tillich by the power of Being-Itself, are made evident in the Christ of the cross—the symbol of the triumph of divine goodness over even the darkest, most hideous, and most depressing kinds of evil in human lives and in the world.

Christ experienced for a time, in his unspeakable agony on the cross, a bleak sense of the total *absence* of the care, support, and presence of God to whom he had dedicated his whole life. This sense is given poignant expression in his mournful cry, "My God, my God, why have you forsaken me?" (Matthew 27: 46). But the Gospel story of Christ's *resurrection* is the story of how the abysmal threats of meaninglessness and evil can be overcome by the unfathomable depths of redemptive goodness, joy, and newness of life.

"Christianity," says Tillich, "is based on this message: God subjects Himself to transitoriness and wrath in order to be with us" (Tillich 1948: 74; see also 61–62). This is his proclamation of the divine kenosis that is also given a central role in the thought of Polkinghorne. But for Polkinghorne, it is the triumphant story of the self-emptying and saving work of a uniquely *existing* and ultimately *personal* God, not that of an inexplicable Being-Itself (Polkinghorne 2000: 125–27).

Rootage of Theological Metaphysics in Revelation

This firm emphasis on God's countless *personal initiatives* and *freely chosen, intentional relationships* with God's human creatures that are recounted throughout the pages of the Hebrew scriptures and those of the Christian New Testament, brings us to Polkinghorne's focus on *divine revelation* as the definitive source and basis of his theological metaphysics: the topic to which we can direct our attention in this section. For Polkinghorne, God is known because God deliberately and continually chooses to make Godself known to humans and in every other aspect of the ongoingness of the world. This is not a God who is merely conjectured and imagined to be such, but a God of personally initiated and continuously reenacted encounters and saving relationships with human beings.

For Polkinghorne, appropriate and adequate theological metaphysics requires the interrelation of two human responses, both turning on what for him constitutes the reality of the "top-down" (1998: 61) revelation of God's nature and of God's works, purpose, and will. The first response is one of "awe and obedience," and "an acceptance of what is given and an appropriate response to the gift" (1998, 60). It is primarily existential, a thankful commitment of the whole of one's life to the deeply felt healing and saving power of the revelation.

But response to revelation also has an important, more purely intellectual side as its recipients strive to understand the meanings of their revelatory experiences, and as some among them devote their lives to inquisitively and conceptually relating such experiences to various other major aspects of thought and life in the world. The latter group consists of *theologians*. Questioning inquiry and critical interpretation are not and should not be confined to professional theologians, however, but should be part of the lives of all who seek for understanding of the revelations and of their applications to life. Acceptance and questioning are thus for Polkinghorne two major requirements of authentic, revelation-based Christian faith (1998, 60–61).

He views the biblical Book of Job as an exemplary exploration of this idea. Job had the courage and conviction to question why God allowed for his terrible, inexplicable suffering. God eventually honored Job's relentlessly questioning spirit with sobering revelation of what it is like to be God. Job's questioning thus finally led to his deeper revelatory awareness of God's character, relations with the world, and with the creatures of the world. In other words, Job had every right and the explicit responsibility to question and inquire into the ways of the self-revealing God in order to gain a more adequate understanding of the relations of God to the sometimes-baffling experiences of tortuous bewilderment and suffering on the part of God's human creatures (1998, 62–63). By his questioning, he made divine revelation truly a part of his own personal awareness and experience.

Theology, as Polkinghorne interprets its character, has an essential conceptual aspect, but it goes awry if it loses sight of its basis in the gracious initiative and gift of divine self-disclosure. He seeks throughout his own theological reflections to maintain a proper balance between these two aspects, but with particular emphasis on what he might be able to contribute intellectually from his own professional area of quantum physics as he earnestly searches for "hints of divinity" in the history of our cosmos (2000, 61).

Natural theology is thus, for him, an important part of the task and challenge of theology as a whole. God reveals Godself, not only in specific acts of manifestation to and communication with particular humans on notable special occasions but also in God's original creation of the orders of nature and their consequent processes of inherent, continuously active natural creativity. The latter call for careful investigation and reflection, not only by natural scientists but also by theologians, and the work of scientists can contribute in important ways, according to Polkinghorne, to theological metaphysics. I will discuss some of his comments in this regard in the next section of this chapter. Revelation and reason, acceptance and questioning, are therefore partners in the theological enterprise. Neither should be neglected, dismissed, or scorned in favor of the other.

In the remainder of this section, in which I am concentrating on Polkinghorne's interpretation of the significance of divine revelation for theological thought, I want to look at two more things. The first is the character of the Hebrew Bible and the Christian New Testament as a record of particular experiences of divine disclosure and revelation testified to by particular humans over many centuries. Here we are brought up against the inescapable fact of *many* purported revelations of religious truth in the various religions of the world and the problem of the *patent differences* among these claimed revelations or experiences of profound religious truth that is posed for the definitive or exclusive truth of any one of them, including the Christian one that relies fundamentally on the Hebrew Bible and the Christian New Testament.

I will refer to this particular record of revelatory experiences simply as *the Bible*, even though it has somewhat different contents for Eastern Orthodox, Roman Catholic, and Protestant Christians. And of course, Jews regard the Hebrew Bible differently and in important and even crucial respects from some of the ways in which Christians view it. This is to say nothing of the many different interpretations Christians have made of its meanings over the centuries of its existence as a complete text. So even the Bible has shown itself to be revelatory for individuals and groups in different, and sometimes fundamentally different, ways.

Which scriptures and whose interpretations of those scriptures? These are always relevant questions to ask about a claimed body of sacred texts. Moreover, one person's or group's interpretive orthodoxy can constitute another group's heresy. The Bible has shown itself to be revelatory for individuals and groups in different, and sometimes fundamentally different ways, and the same is true of other texts regarded as revelatory in different religious traditions. Implicit in these observations is the question of the relations of *specific* claims to disclosure or discovery, on the one hand, and the claimed *universality* of their meanings and truths, on the other—a tension manifested in both religion and natural science.

Particular Revelations and Universal Truth

Polkinghorne is well aware of these two lines of critical reflection about the authority of alleged revelatory texts, including his own Protestant Bible, and we shall want briefly to take note of his reaction to them as a Christian theologian in this section. His appeal to divine revelation as the source and basis of his own Christian faith cannot be insulated against these two problems, as he is well aware. They show that purported authoritative revelations are always subject to the critical tests of the weight and convincingness of particular, finite human traditions, interpretations, and choices. And these are always specific and historically located, even though each of them searches for a calls for commitment to meanings and truths that are claimed to be universal.

Polkinghorne's response to the two problems is also twofold in its basic character. He first lays stress on interpretation as an ongoing historical process, and in the second place, he honestly admits that he does not have a definitive, final answer to either of the problems. His theological metaphysics is an *implicit* "theory of everything," but this metaphysics is admittedly never final or complete. We do the best we can with what is available to us at any given time but even our best efforts and aspirations can never rise to the level of absolute meaning and truth, whether in science or in the field of religion. This is pretty much his response to the second problem, even as he strives to do justice throughout to his faith in the version of the meaning and truth of what he takes to be the essential and universal aspects of the Christian revelation. Surely God is for Polkinghorne the God of all of the peoples of the earth throughout its history, and God's revelations cannot be confined to one people at one time and place.

He is well aware of the problem but confesses that he can offer no new insight into it in his book *Faith, Science, and Understanding* (2000, 65). In his Terry Lectures of 1998, however, he does note that while "Judaism lays its revelatory emphasis on God's dealings with a chosen people, Christianity lays its revelatory emphasis on Christ," and "Islam lays its revelatory emphasis on the infallible message of the Qur'an," this "perplexing diversity pales before the contrast with the religions of Eastern Asia, with many strands of Buddhism appearing not to hold a belief in a deity at all." In his book, he rejects the syncretistic idea that all of the world's religions are basically saying the same thing but also asserts that "despite their many-tongued discourse, the world's religions are at least seeking to speak of a shared encounter with spiritual reality" (1998, 65).

However, his insistence on the historicity of what he takes to be the Christian revelation and of its unfolding interpretations over time, for its part, allows him to make insightful observations about its comparisons with the history of the natural sciences. In doing so, he emphasizes the idea that progress in *approximating* the ideal of absolute meaning and truth is extremely important in its own right, whether in the domain of religion or in the field of the natural sciences.

One obvious example of the Bible's historicity and the limitations of that historicity is the cosmology it assumes in its own times. In biblical times, the earth is assumed to be the center of the universe, and the universe is assumed to have existed for only a short period. The sun and the planets orbit the earth. The idea of a solar system and of that system's place within a vast galaxy, and of that galaxy's being only one of billions of other galaxies in a universe of increasingly extraordinary spatial compass over billions of years of cosmic evolution—these commonly accepted truths of today were totally unknown in the limited period of biblically assumed time and of the Bible's writing.

Natural science can modify the now well-known limitations of both biblical chronology and biblical cosmology in crucial ways, ways that are essential to the Bible's continuing credibility. Its credibility is therefore not fixed in every aspect but subject to significant changes over time, especially those relating to its prescientific aspects and assumptions. The Bible knows nothing of quantum physics or biological evolution, to cite other important examples of the need for updated interpretations of its meanings, and of showing how purported religious revelations are subject to the ongoing need for relevant changes made evident in later times. The need for these changes can be made evident by developments in the natural sciences.

Johannes Kepler discovered that the planets move over elliptical paths, and Galileo Galilei discovered that they orbit the sun, but it required Isaac Newton's later investigations to show *why* their orbits were elliptical by showing that they are continually *falling* around the sun and that their falls are similar to the parabolic paths of balls thrown on the surface of the earth. Galileo never considered Kepler's discovery or thought to ask how it could have been explained. He continued to assume that the paths of the planets were circular, as had long been believed. Shown here is how critical the passage of time is to progress in scientific thought, and how crucial dependence of the scientist on the continual thinking and discovering of the scientist's colleagues is to ongoing progress in science.

The evolution of biological species by natural selection was equally unknown before the time of Darwin and Wallace, and the wide significance of the idea of evolution of all kinds, cosmic, terrestrial, and biological, only came clearly into view later. Quantum physics and the special and general theories of relativity had to await discovery in the twentieth century, and the precise relations among them have yet to be convincingly interpreted and understood. Polkinghorne calls our attention to these and other examples of how historical changes are essential to greater scientific understanding, and how these changes can contribute to a richer and more contemporary understanding of biblical revelation.

He is especially taken, for example, by the developments in his own field of quantum physics and by their implications for understanding the ways of the biblical God. What he interprets to be the evidence for indeterminacy and chance at the quantum level of reality, he also interprets as evidence that the view of God as determining everything that occurs in the universe (*divine omnipotence*) is a resoundingly false idea. God has created the universe, he reasons, with a significant amount of autonomy, and has given scope to responsible autonomy and freedom for God's human creatures.

The idea of divine predestination and total control of everything in the cosmos and human life is thereby shown to be false. God honors our personhood and freedom and does not presume to completely override it. In this way, God relates to us as persons, and not as puppets or automata, showing God's nature to be one of respectful guidance and love, not merely of authoritarian control So once again, science and theology are complements to one another, not opponents to one another, in Polkinghorne's thinking.

As for the long-assumed idea of God's *omniscience*, Polkinghorne observes that since chance and freedom are shown to be real by his professional interpretation of present-day natural science, not only is the future not completely predictable, but it *does not yet exist*, even for God. It is the outcome of time, with its blend of continuity and novelty, meaning that it has yet to become and be real. Contrary to the thought of Isaac Newton, who knew nothing about quantum physics, God cannot know the future in every fine detail because the future does not yet exist, even for God. Nature is not a deterministic machine, as Newton assumed, but a processive system open to genuinely unpredictable kinds of alteration and innovation. And God is not outside time but intimately affected by and involved within it. Polkinghorne associates his comments on divine omnipotence and omniscience with divine kenosis (1998, 126–27).

Finally, Polkinghorne is deeply impressed and inspired by the subtle complexities and multiple orders of nature—some more independent of one another, and others more tightly connected—as these continue to be disclosed by the often startling, continuously unfolding discoveries in natural science. Prior to the twentieth century, for example, physicists were not even sure that there were such things as atoms, and they were ignorant of subatomic phenomena such as electrons, photons, protons, neutrons, neutrinos, gluons, and quarks—to say nothing of positrons and other kinds of so-called antimatter. They were also unaware of dark energy, dark matter, nebula, black holes, and quantum entanglement. Such incredible, continually working and evolving complexity and order give evidence to him of the reality of a personal God ultimately responsible for the creation and order of the ever-changing world. Without God as its creator and sustaining, innovating, guiding presence and ground, Polkinghorne cannot comprehend how such a world could exist. Natural science is therefore revelatory in its own right, and a welcome companion to theological metaphysics.

Relations of the Particular and General

Another issue Polkinghorne brings into view in talking about the interconnections of science and religion is the relations of specific claims to disclosure or discovery, on the one hand, and the implicit universality of their meaning and truth, on the other, as manifested in both religion and natural science. Conveyers or mediators of exceptionally profound and radical new revelatory truths in religion are strikingly rare and quite specific, but this fact does not detract, in Polkinghorne's judgment, from the possible universality of their claims. So the argument that biblical revelations are irreducibly parochial and particular, while scientific claims are general and universal, has no force for him.

The same is true of the developments of natural science from the scientific revolution of the seventeenth century to the present day. Its most notable and profound innovations of thought are introduced and made possible by the particular brilliant inquiring minds of such outstanding scientists as Copernicus, Kepler, Galileo, and Newton, and later, by those of Darwin, Maxwell, Planck, Bohr, Schrödinger, Heisenberg, Einstein, and Dirac. Neither revelation nor science stands still or ever comes to a fixed, unchanging spot, and both depend on the creative insights and experiences of their particular and singularly exemplary figures.

The particular can therefore be, and often has shown itself to be, an opening wedge to the universal. This conviction lies at the heart of Polkinghorne's analysis of divine revelation. God is a God of history, and history is a medium of divine self-disclosure. Nature, or the cosmos, is also such a medium for him, and the history of scientific investigations into it since the seventeenth century brings this conviction forcibly into view. The progressive unfolding of nature's secrets by scientists is part of the meaning of God's continuing revelations throughout history. A good example of this idea is what in contemporary science is called "the cosmological anthropic principle." Polkinghorne finds it to be particularly interesting and important because it relates, not only to the evolution of human persons but to his fundamental conviction of the self-revealing personhood of God. It can also serve as an interesting possible counter to Feuerbach's contention that the idea of a personal God is little more than an anthropomorphic projection.

The Cosmological Anthropic Principle

Scientists are sometimes tempted to make light of or even to deplore the subjective aspects of human experience in their searches for objective, mathematically framed, empirically confirmed truths. The cosmological anthropic principle calls attention, however, to the fact that, in order for humans to have the capability of the high degree of subjective consciousness and awareness characteristic of their species, certain fundamental aspects of nature have had to be extremely fine-tuned. Four examples are Planck's constant that relates the energy of a photon to its frequency, the gravitational constant, the speed of light in a vacuum, and the cosmological constant that relates to the rate of expansion of the universe. Even slight differences in this fine-tuning would have made the evolution of life on earth as we know impossible and, with that, would have prevented the evolution of the human species. Polkinghorne also gives special attention to the central roles of carbon and water to the evolution of life on earth, and to the critical placement of the earth in relation to the radiant energy of the sun. Both factors are essential to the evolution of life (2000, 69–71).

Absences of such fine tuning, available resources, and critical placements would have made impossible, in its turn, such things as scientists and their searches for, and capability of discovering, formulating, and empirically confirming objective truths. Without subjectivity there could be no such thing as objectivity in scientific thought or elsewhere. Therefore there would be no such thing as the evolution of the cosmos as we have come to know it, no evolution of life, no evolution of human life, and no such thing as science or scientists apart from the cosmological anthropic principle in its various guises.

Polkinghorne takes this principle seriously and regards the fact of it as evidence for God's creation and maintenance of the world, a world that, here on earth, has made life, conscious life forms, human life and culture, scientists, and the enterprise of natural science itself possible. In allowing for the evolution of humans on earth, it can also give evidence for the role of humans being—like Polkinghorne's conception of the ultimate nature of God—*persons* in their own right, God's representatives on earth made in God's image, and responsible custodians of ecological health and well-being on earth.

The only alternative to the cosmological anthropic principle Polkinghorne can envision is the "many worlds" thesis, according to which this world is only one of many worlds and just *happens* to be the one in which such fine-tuning or availability of critical resources and placements is present. In his view, the many-worlds thesis is extravagant, ad-hoc, and implausible. The more convincing thesis is that God has intentionally created the world in this way. Here, for him, is evidence of the complementary character of natural science and divine revelation (1998, 85–89).

Critical Comments

I applaud Polkinghorne's endeavor to break down the barrier that is sometimes, if not often, thought to stand between religion and natural science. He does an admirable job in this respect, showing how, in his view, each can contribute to the intelligibility and plausibility of the other.

He does this particularly as a Christian theologian and quantum physicist. But I must take issue with his conception of theology as being a *metaphysics* within which all of the other aspects of human life and culture are encompassed. For one thing, religion is larger than theology because not all religions are theistic. But even more importantly, metaphysics as I understand it is the search for a general perspective on the contributions and interrelations of all of the major dimensions of life and human culture. These include religion, art, morality, philosophy, history, politics, the natural and social sciences, and technology—in a word, all of the major dimensions of the world and of life in the world, including the daily lives and experiences of each human being. Religion is a part of metaphysics as I interpret its task, but only a part, and theology is only one kind of religious outlook and reflection.

Polkinghorne is well within his rights, however, in thinking that Christian theology has throughout its history regarded God as a real, living person. He has endorsed this view of God and is thus able to conceive of God as personal creator of the universe, personally involved in the affairs of earth as active agent, entering into personal relations of saving judgment, mercy, and love with God's human creatures, and the like. In doing so, he is also careful to take issue with the "omni" attributes often associated with God in traditional Christianity, showing that these are incompatible with God's respect for the freedom of humans and the important autonomous functions God has given to nature as a whole. God is not just a God of all-knowing control, dominating the universe and human lives from a place outside of time, but a God of active involvement in human history and human affairs.

For Polkinghorne, as for Christians through the ages, the nature of God is most fully and intimately revealed in the person of Jesus the Christ, where God shares in the lives of finite human beings by becoming one of them and reveals Godself to be a God of suffering mercy, forgiveness, salvation, and love. This saving message and image of divine love lies at the heart of Polkinghorne's Christianity, as it has for Christianity since its early years. Polkinghorne's God is a God of self-revelation, not just of human imagination or conceptualization, but he also seeks to do justice to natural theology and to draw, in doing so, on his own scientific field of quantum physics to show how it can give new avenues of access to Christian theology as he conceives it. His scientific experiences and reflections add in this manner to the overall picture of Christianity he shares with Kierkegaard and Tillich. In strongly endorsing the idea of God as a person who is actively involved in human history, he also shows himself to be in agreement with Buber's thesis about the ongoing "I-thou" relationship of humans with God.

I find much to ponder in the thought of Tillich, although I also disagree with it in some ways. Tillich does an extremely good job of illuminating the existential, and not merely the conceptual, aspects of lived religion. Most particularly, however, and as I will show later in this book, I do *not think* that nature as a whole requires some non-natural or supernatural *ground*. My "Being-Itself" is nature, not God. The natural is the real and the whole of the real, and it is pervaded with religious meaning and salvific import in its own right. Thus, nature, in my judgment, *is its own ground*, and for me it is *sacred ground*.

Moreover, I find in my fellow humans as well as in the community of nonhuman sentient beings on the face of the earth, a multiplicity of "thous" with whom it is extremely important for me and all of us humans to enter into as many intimate, caring, mutually helpful relationships as possible. This conviction has especially poignant and pressing significance in our time of imminent ecological crisis on earth.

Tillich in the mid-twentieth century already anticipated this present crisis and the dire need for a kind of I-thou relationship of human beings with the innumerable other nonhuman "thous" of nature.[1] In a sermon preached partly on the text of the New Testament book of Romans, the last verse of which states, "For we know that the whole creation groaneth and travaileth in pain together until now" (Romans 8: 22), Tillich remarks, "This technical civilization, the pride of mankind, has brought about a tremendous devastation of original nature, of the land, of animals, of plants. It has kept genuine nature in small reservations and has occupied everything for domination and ruthless exploitation." He then adds, "And worse: many of us have lost the ability to live with nature. We fill it with the noise of empty talk, instead of listening to it many voices, and through them, to the voiceless music of the universe" (1946, 79). This is the kind of voiced and voiceless I-thou discourse and relationship I can heartily endorse. And it is pregnant with religious meaning.

Polkinghorne helps to flesh out this Tillichian picture of a nature that is sacred and sufficient in and of itself with his marvelous scientific explorations of the extraordinary depths, complexities, and capabilities of nature that are being brought into clearer focus by today's natural science. His appeal is to something radically more than nature, while mine is entirely to a wondrous, self-sufficient, continuously creative natural order of which I am privileged to be a part. So he and I are in partial important agreement and in partial important disagreement in our visions of reality and human existence. For him, as for me, science contributes in significant ways to religion and to a profound religious empathy with the whole of nature. But it cannot substitute for a religious approach to nature for either of us.

Conclusion

So far in this book, I have concentrated on the stimulating ideas of different thinkers regarding the question of the existence of God, the nature of God, and God's relationship to human beings. I have done so by examining aspects of the thought of Kierkegaard, Buber, Tillich, Feuerbach, Schilling, and Polkinghorne, as well as interjecting my own personal views along the way. Our journey is far from complete, as we continue our search for what, if anything, can be said to lie *beyond God* in religious, as well as philosophical, scientific, and other major interpretations of nature, the innumerable forms of life on earth, and the unending quest for existential meaning.

Whether or not there is a fundamental religious dimension to life on earth, there is plenteous, and sometimes overbearing suffering, anxiety, and sense of hopelessness here. Without the aid of the religious dimension it can all come to look bleak, pointless, and full of despair for finite beings such as we humans. We need the power of religion to help give us sustaining confidence and hope, or what Tillich wisely calls "the courage to be." He is right about this, and Dawkins is wrong. Natural science alone cannot save us. "But what kind of religion: theistic or non-Theistic?" That is the question that will continue to occupy us throughout the remainder of this book.

Chapter Six

The Probability of Monotheism

How probable or believable is the theistic hypothesis as a way of explaining the origin and character of the world as we presently experience it? British philosophical theologian Richard Swinburne argues that the theistic hypothesis is both the simplest and the most probable way of explaining why the cosmos and everything in it exist as we experience them. By *theism*, he has in mind the monotheism of the Christian tradition, of which he is a firm defender. But he mainly intends his arguments in the second edition of his book *The Existence of God* (2004) to apply to a more generic monotheism or what he calls "bare theism" (2004, 265–66) as the most promising and convincing way of explaining the existence of the world and our experiences of the world.

I shall first present in an expository manner, and in consecutive sections, the following aspects of Swinburne's defense of monotheism: his concept of God and his allegation that the existence, character, and role of God as so described provide the simplest and most probable explanation for the existence of the world and for its basic aspects as brought to light by contemporary science; his contention that this theistic explanation extends to the world's teleological, moral, and aesthetic aspects; that it has a strong rootage in religious experience; and that it accounts for the multitudinous forms of life on earth as preparatory for the evolution of humans, for their separate conscious minds being joined in Cartesian or dualistic fashion to their physical bodies, and for their relationships as spiritual beings with a purely spiritual God in this life and in a life to come beyond the grave. Finally, I shall provide a brief summary of Swinburne's attempted resolution of the problem posed by the existence of so much natural evil and humanly caused and tolerated moral evil in a world he believes to be created and sustained by a God of perfect moral goodness.

Following these expository sections, I shall offer a critical discussion of Swinburne's arguments in support of their particular claims. I will not be able in a brief chapter to do justice to every aspect of Swinburne's lengthy and often highly detailed discussions of these and other matters. I can only survey some of their high points. But my doing so will give us another useful and provocative perspective on theological and philosophical ways of looking at the monotheistic hypothesis.

The expositions and critical discussions of this chapter will conclude the major ways in which I have approached constructive arguments for theism—or, more specifically, monotheism—as these have been set forth by Kierkegaard, Buber, Tillich, Schelling, Polkinghorne, and Swinburne. They also bring into important critical contrast the case against theism mounted by Feuerbach. The remainder of this book will be devoted to lines of argument that call into fundamental question theistic supernaturalism and supernaturalisms of any kind. They will defend a version of religious naturalism in which *nature* in its many aspects and *as its own ground* is held to be the ultimate metaphysical reality and most appropriate focus of religious faith, commitment, and concern.

Swinburne's Concept of God

Swinburne defends a traditional and commonly assumed conception of God but also seeks to show its continuing vital relevance for the contemporary world. He argues that God is a disembodied pure spirit, that God is omnipotent, omniscient, and omnipresent, that God is perfectly good, that God is one person, and that God is perfectly free and thus not constrained by the past or by anxiety about the future in the way that all of God's creatures are, including us humans.

Swinburne also argues that God exists necessarily in the sense that it would be impossible for God not to exist and that belief in God's necessary existence provides the simplest and most probable ultimate explanation and basis for the existence of what he regards as the contingent natural world and everything in it. The explanations of the natural sciences are penultimate and incomplete. The probability of an extremely complex world with all of its intricately related aspects existing without God is considerably lower than the probability of one existing with God as its creator and sustainer. Belief in God makes sense out of the world and of our place within the world in a way that the absence of such belief does not and cannot. It gives us a ground for our existence and that of the world itself, and its ground is an inviolable *saving* ground for our finite, fallible existence in a manner similar to that argued for by Tillich.

God and the Teleological, Moral, and Aesthetic Aspects of Experience

Swinburne is convinced that the character and role of God in relation to the world provide the best explanation for the teleological (purposive or goal-oriented), moral, and aesthetic aspects of human experience, as well as giving comprehensive purpose and meaning to the world as a whole and to our own lives as participants in the world.

As the creation of a conscious, purposeful divine being, the world is replete with evidences of its purposive origin and maintenance. It gives every evidence of being the creation of God and of being constantly guided and sustained by God. It does not just exist as a brute, inexplicable fact. Its intricacy, complexity, and fine-tuned wonder, as brought so clearly into focus by the natural sciences, cry out for explanation. Swinburne's repeated emphasis on the anthropic fine-tuning of nature (172–88) reminds us of Polkinghorne's similar emphasis.

Equipage of the earth's living creatures with the in-built capacities of adaptation and survival that are so common to all of them in their enormous range of types and numbers gives evidence of its own to their having been created, or more properly, *arranged to be created through evolution*, by God. Drawing distinctions between moral good and evil has its ultimate rootage in animal awareness of what is best or worst for its adaptive needs and survival, and those of its progeny. At some point in the evolutionary process, its outcomes are creatures able to judge the truth and falsity of implicit, if not explicit, moral claims (212–18). Moral consciousness develops with the development of consciousness itself, and its ultimate source and explanation lies in the existence of an exquisitely righteous, merciful, moral, and dependable, agential God.

Finally, God loves beauty. This fact accounts ultimately for the beauty of the earth, for that of its multifarious creatures, and for the acute sensitivity to beauty on the part of God's human creatures. What philosopher F. R. Tennant calls the "superfluity" of beauty across the face of the earth and cites as compelling evidence for the existence of God (Tennant: 92–93) is for him, as well as for Swinburne, attestation to the beauty of divine holiness and the ardent cherishing of beauty everywhere and everywhen commonly and rightly attributed to God. God is not only wondrously beautiful in Godself, God treasures and admires all things beautiful. So the presence on earth and in its creatures of so much astounding beauty is in itself ample evidence for the existence of God. Our human attunement to beauty is evidence, in its turn, of our kinship with God.

Biological Evolution, Human Mind-Body Dualism, and the Afterlife

Instead of viewing mind as something that results entirely from the evolution of life on earth and has its ultimate basis in the interworkings of matter-energy and time, Swinburne views mind or spiritual substance as a separate kind of reality that is somehow attached to human beings and their material bodies by God. Our possession of mind gives to us a spiritual aspect akin to the pure spirituality of God. Swinburne thus heartily endorses a version of René Descartes's mind-body dualism, despite all of the relevant objections mounted against it by philosophers who were contemporary with and came after Descartes. The most serious objection is that two radically different presumed substances such as mind and body would have no natural connections with one another. It is not at all clear, therefore, how each could influence the other, or even how mind or spirit could somehow be "located" in the physical body of a human being or any other biological organism.

But Swinburne argues that God has created these two substances—physical and mental—and arranged for their interrelations by attaching the one to the other at some phase of the process of biological evolution, starting with animals thus endowed with minimal consciousness and proceeding to the evolution of those with higher degrees of conscious awareness and intentional capability. This process culminates in human beings and does so primarily because God has arranged the process of evolution to produce beings akin in their capabilities and powers—although only finitely and fallibly akin—to God's own personhood and nature. God could then enjoy companionship with these human beings to an extent and in ways not possible with the nonhuman, less fully conscious and aware creatures of nature.

Our possession of minds as humans marks us as *ensouled*, as having spiritual selves in bodies but that are not ultimately explicable solely in terms of bodily processes. In fact, Swinburne even argues that there is no way in which scientists will ever be able to explain how physical processes alone can give rise to mental or spiritual natures and capabilities. He states that

> because we have every reason to believe that there can be no scientific theory and so scientific laws correlating brain states with souls and their states, we have every reason to believe that the causal connections that exist between them do not have a scientific explanation in terms of the properties of brain states; they are additional causal connections independent of the set of scientific laws governing the physical world. Nothing about the physical world makes it in the very least probable that there would be these connections. (210)

According to Swinburne, an uncaused, sheerly given, extremely complex, finely tuned world of the sort we humans find ourselves living in day-by-day is extremely unlikely. The infinite power and completely unconstrained intentions and choices of a personal, rational, all-knowing God are required for an adequate, truly persuasive explanation for its existence. The world gives every evidence of coming into being and evolving to its present state, not by accident or chance, but by realization of the deliberate choices and planning of God.

In arguing for the insufficiency of even the best scientific explanations to account for biological evolution, and especially for the extreme fine-tuning necessary for the origination of life and the evolution of human beings, Swinburne makes common cause, as I mentioned earlier, with Polkinghorne's reasoning for the existence of God. Their reasoning seems to be something like this: explanation by means of intentional actions of a conscious agent is simpler, more convincing, and more probable in most cases than basing them ultimately on purely contingent or accidental factors. The more intricate and complex the thing to be explained is, the more compelling this line of reasoning is likely to be. A blind watchmaker is much less likely than a conscious, intelligent, fully aware one. The point holds emphatically and most convincingly for Swinburne when applied to the universe.

Swinburne expands on this argument at one place in his book by contending that if the universe is of finite age, that is, having had some kind of absolute beginning in the past, or if it is of infinite age, meaning that it consists of an infinite collection of past series of facts, each existing for a finite period of time, the universe's existence in either case is "an inexplicable brute fact" and something "far too big" for science to explain (142).

In other words, far from being the basis of all explanation, as many scientists and others (including me) may be strongly inclined to believe, nature for Swinburne requires a basis *beyond itself*. Its simplest and most probable basis is a personal monotheistic God as its ultimate conceiver, creator, and sustainer. He dismisses religious naturalism out of hand, as he does the metaphysics of scientific naturalism.

Nature for Swinburne is not enough. It cannot be its own ground. God is required to account for the whole of nature and for us humans on earth and our experiences as crucial parts of it. By means of biological evolution and the souls God attaches to it at various points, God endows humans with reasoning capacities sufficient for them to recognize and affirm God's existence as implicit in their having come into being as an acutely conscious, highly intelligent species of life.

Swinburne even suggests that God creates the world with the primary purpose of bringing into existence by evolution creatures such as ourselves, creatures that can freely choose and enter into spiritual fellowship and communion with their creator, and even continue to do so eventually in an everlasting afterlife rid of the constraints, fallibilities, and anxieties of finite, mortal, merely physical existence. As a God of compassion and love, God yearns for loving companionship with God's human creatures, creatures with the freedom and mental capacity to love God intentionally and actively in return (119).

Swinburne's focus throughout his discussions seems to be on planet earth and ensouled humans on the face of this planet. His arguments tend, therefore, to have a kind of parochial, principally earth-centered ring, although he clearly intends for them to extend to the cosmos as a whole. I'll return to this point when I get to my critical comments on Swinburne's conception of God and his arguments for God's existence.

Religious Experience and Commitment to God

Swinburne also argues that belief in the existence of a personal God and commitment to the basic traits he associates with the conception of God have profound rootage in religious experience, and especially in the revelatory experiences of the great religious teachers, prophets, and exemplars of monotheistic faith. This faith for him, therefore, is a fundamentally experiential and not just a conceptual or purely epistemic outlook on God and the world. As such, it is also profoundly *existential*, bearing in fundamental ways on the most pressing, desperately important issues and concerns of human life—issues to which divine revelation speaks in profound and saving ways.

Swinburne is especially careful to supplement his philosophical arguments with occasional specific attention to Christian monotheism as he interprets and understands it and its basis in putative divine revelations or self-disclosures (see, for example, 288–92). For him, it is reasonable to expect that God would not just leave us with intellectual speculations about God's existence, nature, and will, but would also provide us with

God's specific communications concerning them: communications growing out of and giving purpose and direction to our ongoing relations with God. These relations, which have importance and reality in meaningful and transformative religious life, are given strong emphasis in the writings of Martin Buber and reflected in the other theologians whose writings are discussed in this book's earlier chapters.

Swinburne is very much in Buber's camp at heart. His God is ultimately a God of revelatory self-disclosure and loving relationships, not just a God of philosophy and abstract reason. I respect and honor his faith, even though I do not share in its most important aspect: namely, his focus on God and his confident arguments concerning the characteristics of God and the alleged extreme simplicity and high probability of God's existence as so described.

The Problem of Evil

Swinburne is convinced that God loves the world of God's creation, and that God especially loves human beings. But in order to be in loving relationship with human beings, they must learn how to love God in return, and they must freely choose to do so. Love cannot be forced or commanded; it must be freely given, and it requires traits of character to be willingly developed over the course of time. One must learn how to love and how most effectively to love, and how to do so in the face of significant aspects of adversity and trial.

Were there no evils of suffering and pain, there would be no need for compassion toward those who suffer and no lessons of patience and continuing faith in divine power and goodness in the presence of one's own sufferings or those of loved ones close by. And if the existence of God were perfectly obvious to all and did not need constant testing, reaffirmation, and works of love toward God and others in the world— human and nonhuman—then one would be so habituated to divine love as to take it for granted and not to aspire throughout one's life to learn how to love God in return.

Moreover, the whole story of biological evolution is the story of how natural organisms must struggle toward successful adaptations to their natural environments and how they attain sufficient strength, resiliency, and knowledge to do so. Their very existence as species of life in their care for progeny (when the progeny remain close by after their birth), the maintenance and protection of their own lives, and their learning necessary, life-saving lessons of cause and effect depend on their ability to cope with natural evils or the threats of their surrounding environments to their thriving and surviving. As outcomes of biological evolution in ways ordained by God, humans must also expect themselves to be a part of such natural processes of acclimatization and fitness.

And as social beings, humans must also be prepared for trials and tribulations inflicted on the helpless and weak by the misguided or malicious choices of other humans. The price of the lessons of freedom and love for humans, if these are to be real in God's created world, are a significant number of evils, both natural and moral. And we should not expect it to be otherwise. This is Swinburne's basic conclusion in response to the problem of evil and the serious threat it might seem to pose for the existence of a gracious, loving, perfectly moral God. The motto of the British Royal Air Force, *per ardua ad astra*, seems to me to be a fitting summary of his point of view.

Critical Response to These Arguments

In arguing that the monotheistic hypothesis is far and away the simplest and most probable explanation for the existence of the universe and everything in it, including us human beings, Swinburne seems to be oblivious to the possibility that this is anything but obviously and most simply the case. He seems to have at least partly in mind the idea that attributing the existence of something to an intentional, personal creator or agent responsible for that something is more convincing by far than thinking of it as having always existed in some shape or form rather than being created de novo, or as always having had some inherent character or potentiality rather than deriving it from outside itself.

In the former case, all new kinds of existence would be the result of transformations of older ones, and there need not be an absolute beginning of the whole process. This explanation would apply to the evolution of the present universe by means of an original colossal burst of energy (perhaps produced out of the debris of a previously collapsed universe), the consequent immediate outcome of some sort of plasma, the emergence of subatomic particles, forces, and fields from that plasma, their transformations and organizations into atoms of many kinds, then atoms into molecules, the evolution of life and of more complex forms of life from such molecules—especially the RNA and DNA molecules—and then on to the emergence of conscious organisms and the development, when appropriate, of their various simple and then more complex cultures, and finally, to human beings and their highly sophisticated cultural creations here on earth and, in all probability, something pervasively similar elsewhere in the vast present cosmos.

There need not be anything like an original conscious designer or guide involved in such completely natural processes of transformation and change. Consciousness, intentionality, and culture result from them rather than preceding them. And these are emergent functions of matter-energy, not something nonbodily or nonphysical somehow externally attached to them at a later stage of evolutionary development.

The primordial existence of matter-energy, interacting with the influences of the continuities and novelties of primordial time, can thus be sufficient to explain the existence of our universe as we presently live in it and have come to understand it. This understanding could include awareness of and response to its inherent moral and aesthetic values, as well as accounting for the purposive behaviors of all organisms, especially the more complex ones. In this case, purposiveness can be understood as an essential *part of the process* whereby biological organisms adapt to their physical and social environments. And this observation would apply as much to human organisms as to any other ones.

Such a mode of explanation is at least as simple and probable as the theistic one, and it has the virtue of being close to the current scientific understanding of such matters. It does not require that there be anything like a primordial purpose involved in the origin of the universe; it proposes instead that purpose, value, and meaning—intellectual, moral, aesthetic, and religious—are emergent factors within it. This is a radically *incarnational* or entirely *physicalist* outlook. It requires no need to posit mind-body dualism and no purely spiritual divine being said somehow to create and interact with a physical world.

Swinburne therefore fails to convince me that a God of omni-attributes provides us with the simplest and most probable explanation for the existence and present character of the universe, or of our place as humans within it. It is not at all clear to me, for example, how God can be a distinctive personal being and yet be present everywhere in the incredibly vast universe and have detailed awareness of what is happening everywhere at all times, even down to the secret thoughts and firsthand experiences of every human being, to say nothing of the other species of life that have evolved to have consciousness in various degrees. It is not at all clear to me how such a God could bring the universe into existence in the first place. Nor is it clear to me how this single personal God continues to order, guide, regulate, and sustain the incredibly complex, multi-faceted, ever-expanding universe in being.

I get no clear, simple, probable picture from Swinburne's descriptions of God of how God can be immense enough and yet believable enough to encompass, order, and direct the affairs and highly probable living and consciously living experiences elsewhere in an incredibly enormous universe of billions of galaxies, stars, and planets. Most of his discussions of God and God's relations to the world seem to be primarily about events and experiences of this earth, a fact that gives them a parochial, limited, quaintly first-century ring.

We are scientifically in the first stages of trying to understand how the present universe came into being, what the fundamental subatomic particles, fields, and forces are and how they can be explained, how general relativity and quantum physics can be reconciled or supplanted by newer and more adequate theories, what is going on beyond the earth and its solar system, what dark energy and dark matter are and how their roles in the universe can be interpreted and explained, what the future of this universe will be like—especially as it expands beyond our ability to receive light signals from its most distant reaches, whether the universe had an absolute beginning, whether our present universe is the only one, and so on.

And, of course, the future may bring substantial alterations of presently assumed scientific understanding that we cannot in the present even begin to imagine. Explaining everything by means of a traditional, omni-attributed God seems to me to be much too facile and frustratingly *ad hoc* to be convincing.

I favor explaining things by means of or in terms of the universe rather than trying to explain the universe itself with something completely distinct from it, especially a distinct something that, Feuerbach reminds us, looks suspiciously like us humans raised to an incomprehensible degree. In any event, defending the existence, nature, and role of an omni-attributed God—in and of itself—strikes me as being a far more formidable task than Swinburne makes it out to be. I am not persuaded by his insistence that it is simpler and more probable than any other possible explanation of everything else, or by his arguments to this effect. To explain the whole of nature by means of something entirely nonnatural, purely spiritual, and entirely nonphysical seems to me to be a futile enterprise, or at least one that I see no need of.

Swinburne argues that morality, beauty, and the intelligibility of the universe require explanation beyond the universe itself. But for me, the roots of all three of these reside in nature itself and are explicable in naturalistic terms. Without agreed-upon moral principles, no human society could long exist. God is not required to explain their existence. Beauty of extraordinarily diverse and enchanting kinds is present throughout nature, as our human aesthetic sensitivities continuously inform us and inspire us. This beauty is not superfluous in nature but an integral part of nature's immanent workability, wonder, and glory. Were the universe not intelligible in and of itself, there would be no knowledge of it essential to survival in it, and no such thing as credible natural science or even technology of the simplest sort. Nature is its own ground in all of its manifestations, both now and in the distant and probably everlasting past. It does not require some ground outside of and beyond itself. This thesis is at least as credible, if not more so, than the thesis of its creation and sustenance by a God of incomprehensible omni-attributes.

So-called natural evils result from the many-ordered, continually changing character of the natural world. Its focus is clearly not entirely on us humans and our well-being, nor is it even on all of the nonhuman forms of life on earth. We humans are caught in intricate webs of interdependence that can make our lives perilous in one aspect and prosperous in another. At any rate, *it's not all about us!* As beings gifted with significant amounts of personal freedom, we are capable of inflicting grievous harm as well as of working toward gracious good in our relations with one another and other aspects of earthly life and nonlife.

But what about religious experience? Does it not give persuasive evidence of the existence of God and of God's bringing the universe into being and sustaining it in its being? Swinburne is convinced that it does. But religious experience through the ages and in all human cultures to date does not show unanimity of conviction about its sources or meanings. There are monotheistic and polytheistic religions, for example, and there are nontheistic ones. There are religions in which nature, not some sort of deity or collection of deities, is the focus. Claimed revelations are many and diverse. Religious experiences have certainly been evident throughout human history, showing the importance of religious belief, thought, and commitment for human beings. But they have provided few if any unequivocal religious truths other than that of the need to attend carefully to manifestations of the sacred in their myriad forms.

What Swinburne, as a monotheistic Christian takes for granted is not the significance of religious experience for all. He is right in assuming that if God is as he describes God to be, namely a personal being who yearns for fellowship with God's human creatures, then it makes sense to assume that a loving God would reach out to and seek to enter into relationship with them—thus providing to them essential information about God's nature, purposes, and will. But this reasoning stems from assumptions about the one God and the nature of the one God that are not held by all of the world's religions or thought to be implicit in their forms of religious experience.

Swinburne's assumption of mind-body or spirit-matter dualism causes problems for his conception of the nature of God and for his conception of humans in their relations to God. It is not at all clear how a purely spiritual God could relate to the physical universe and its physical creatures. And the notion that minds are somehow *attached to* humans and other conscious creatures rather than being evolved from and being functions of matter-energy leaves us with the question of how these minds could be affected by, affect, or relate in any meaningful way to material brains, nervous systems, or other aspects of complex human bodies. Nor is it clear how they could be implanted in and made resident within those bodies. If there are no inherent linkages or commonalities of spirit and body, how would a relationship with the two of them be possible or explicable, established or maintained?

The absence of a physical body in God's case allows God, in Swinburne's judgment, to be free of the restrictions of bodily existence and of those of ordinary spatial-temporal existence, but they somehow also allow God to choose to become human and suffer the temptations, anxieties, afflictions, and trials of embodied human existence in the person of Jesus the Christ—while still remaining the alleged God of pure spirit. It is not clear how this could be possible. To insist that nothing is impossible for God provides no convincing answer to such questions, especially in light of Swinburne's insistence that not even God can do something that is logically impossible (2004, 94, 98). Since God is not outside of time but everlasting within time, God cannot know the future because the future does not yet exist (80, n. 5). I applaud him for this insightful recognition. But he gives me no insight about how purely spiritual minds can locate within and operate freely and effectively within physical systems such as the human body.

The notion, moreover, that humans are fundamentally spiritual beings temporarily encased in human bodies gives credence to Swinburne's conviction that this notion permits them to be conceived as being created in the image of God and destined for a true home beyond nature in a spiritual realm viewed also as God's true home. Here, in their resurrected state, they will have bodies still, but these bodies will be incorruptible and so profoundly different from their former bodies on earth. Implicit in this eschatological vision is the idea that the earth or the physical universe cannot be conceived as the true home of God's human creatures. That home is heaven, and abiding there everlastingly with God will be in some kind of entirely different "body" immune to all of the limitations, fallibilities, frustrations, and dangers of their former bodily existence.

But will they still be free? If not, they have become robots rather than persons. But if so, can they then be, or should they be, forever insulated against the possibility of misusing their freedom or of needing continuously to learn from its misuses? A deeper question implicit in this heavenly scenario is whether it would be possible for them to rebel against God and bring about a new exile from their heavenly paradise as the consequence of new acts of disobedience to God. Something like this allegedly occurred with the myth of Satan and his minions being hurled out of heaven because of their radical disobedience to God.

Along with the question of continuing freedom in the afterlife is the more general question of how, in their risen, incorruptible bodies, they could still be the *same persons* as they were on earth, namely, finite without still being fallible, eternally and contentedly at rest without needing to be challenged and to struggle, satisfied with their risen lot without their ongoing contributions being important or needed in an already perfect mode of existing, having no need to learn because everything essential for their life will already be known, not further relied upon and not needed because everything is already perfect—is all of this really different from being in *hell*, for creatures such as we are here on earth? There are no everlasting tortuous flames, but there is also no clear motivation or reason to exist forever.

Most fundamentally, in my view, implicit in the hope of heaven are three other problems Swinburne does not address or for which he has no clear answer. The first problem is an implicit denigration of earthly existence; the second one is the idea of heaven as recompense for all the toils, agonies, sufferings, and injustices of earthly human existence. Can there be such a thing as a satisfying, reassuring, everlasting recompense for the Holocaust? And the third one is the inevitability of death for all of God's supposed creatures other than God's human ones—a scenario that includes the most fully conscious other ones that are, like humans, outcomes of biological evolution.

Earth and its future pale in comparison with the hope of heaven for humans. If it is not their true home, a possible implication is that they need not concern themselves much with its future. This attitude could turn out to be disastrous for its future in view of the ways in which human beings have placed its future and that of its nonhuman life forms in peril in a time of ecological crisis. The second problem is the hope of heaven as recompense for the evils humans have brought about in their history can be interpreted to minimize the seriousness of those evils and of future ones to come—and thus of the problem of an assumed perfect moral goodness of the God who has allowed them to occur.

The third problem is that if humans alone out of all of the earth's creatures are not doomed to final death and nonexistence, the implication is that they alone matter enough to have their lives preserved forever. This conviction runs against the grain of all ecological insistence on the interdependence of all of earth's biologically evolved creatures, and the essential role death plays to ensure that no one species of life be exempt from the common fates of death that must apply to all of them if the earth's carrying capacity for life is not to be quickly overrun.

This point is especially telling, given Swinburne's recognition that humans, like all of the life forms on earth, are divinely intended products of biological evolution, not specially created ones at some instantaneous point in the past. Biology, life, death, and radical interdependence are closely entwined conceptions, while the hope of an everlasting afterlife for members of the human species alone seems to be a jarring, incoherent exception.

There is a picture of a basket of newborn puppies above my desk. I have no reason to suppose that their lives are meaningless if they are fated someday to die, as assuredly they are. If I am fated to be immortal or to have some kind of resurrection from the dead, why should they not as well? The gift of a finite life is precious and should be prized, even though it does not last forever. And it is essential for all biological organisms that it be so. It is the necessary price each of them must pay for the ongoing life of the whole ecosystem of the earth. It is an incalculable privilege to be here on earth, even if only for a while. We should cherish and explore its possibilities for good, for ourselves and for others, while we live and not concern ourselves too much with what, if anything, might lie beyond the grave. And we should not exempt ourselves from the fate of other living beings on earth.

But what about the question of the purpose of the universe and of life within it? Can we conceive of such without belief in a purposive divine creator? Apart from God, how could the urgent question of our own purpose for existing be given a meaningful answer? I hold that purpose is emergent rather than primordial, and that it emerges with the evolution of purposive beings. Thus, there are purposes aplenty here on earth, whether or not there is some purpose for the existence of earth itself.

Every living being exhibits purposes, whether consciously intended as such or not. Such purposes subserve the maintenance of life and of the kind of and quality appropriate to each distinctive form of life. But there need not be any antecedent cosmic purpose for purposive activities and recognitions eventually to come into being. A panpsychist hypothesis is not required. Psyche or mind is an outcome and feature of life, not the precondition for it. It can be accounted for in naturalistic ways. A theistic way is not required (for a book-length defense of this counter to panpsychism, see Crosby 2023).

Finally and perhaps most importantly, what Swinburne does not consider, with his God of omni-attributes, is the idea that the problem of evil is in a way a more serious problem *for God* than it is for human beings. God, as he envisions God, has created humans with the gift of substantial freedom in the hope that they would devote their freedom to loving concern for one another, for the natural order and it nonhuman creatures of which they are a part, and for their divine creator. But they have failed God in all three respects, and to a disastrous degree. This must cause God calamitous suffering, grief, and disappointment—which is given poignant expression in the suffering of Jesus on the cross—a suffering willfully inflicted on God, at least symbolically, by hateful humanity. The God conventionally seen as a God of secure power, presence, and control, if not in the immediate present, at least in the triumphant future that God is trusted eventually to bring into being, is a God who must rely on his human creatures to help God bring about.

So long as humans are truly free, this future cannot be guaranteed. God's hope and man's hope are inseparably conjoined. They either win together, or they both lose. Seen from this angle of interpretation, the suffering of Jesus the Christ on the cross at Golgotha is manifestation of God's bitter disappointment at humans' failure to give to one another, to nature, and to God the love and acceptance that God passionately craves. God, seen in this manner, is not so much the triumphant, all-powerful, self-sufficient leader as the patiently waiting father of the prodigal son—desperate in his intensely mourning and suffering hope for the son's return. This is a God of absolutely self-limiting love, not a God of absolute any other thing. I do not believe that Swinburne as a Christian can have it both ways.

Conclusion

Richard Swinburne mounts an impressive, richly detailed case for the existence of a monotheistic God. His arguments in this regard are often subtle and far-reaching. But they do not, in the final analysis, convince me that the God of his allegations, descriptions, and reasonings must exist, or that the claim to God's existence is the simplest and most probable explanation for the existence of the universe or for the point and purpose of our existence as human beings on the face of the earth. He seems to me to assume more than he successively proves. Perhaps all arguments of this type do so, including those I develop and present in the present book.

At some major junctions in reasoning about religious matters, we give expression to a religious faith that lies *at the basis* of our reasoning rather than being its clear or incontestable *outcome*. It is extremely important, nevertheless, that we commit our best efforts to thinking critically about that faith in order to give both rational and empirical support to it, especially as we enter into dialogue with others about central existential issues of life and meaning. Our judgments about simplicity and probability relating to such reasonings will vary with the strengths of faiths to which the reasonings give expression. This is not to say that faith is arbitrary. It is only to point out that reasonable faith and faithful reasoning are intricately conjoined (see Crosby 2011). This is only as it should be, given the magnitude and depth of the visions and perplexities under consideration.

We assuredly need the help and guidance of the great religious teachers of the many different religious traditions in our own struggles toward reasonable, truly convincing forms of faith. But there is no such thing as absolute, unassailable, unquestionable authority in such matters. And we should be deeply suspicious of anyone or any point of view, text, institution, or person that lays claim to such absolute religious authority.

As Swinburne rightly insists, we are free, and with that freedom comes the responsibility to subject religious claims—whether those of sacred scriptures, established religious traditions and institutions, or charismatic teachers and exemplars—to the test of our personal lives, thinking, and experience. We must critically question, interpret, and apply their claims to our lives if such claims are to have orienting, transformative, saving meaning for our lives. But we can also do so in gratitude for what they offer us in the way of possible truth, seasoned understanding, and wisdom. I express my gratitude here for the faithful reasoning of Kierkegaard, Buber, Tillich, Schelling, Polkinghorne, and Swinburne, and, yes, also Feuerbach, for the stimulus they have given to my own thinking and I hope also to my readers' own. Because the title of this book is *Beyond Monotheism*, I want now to give explicit development and defense of my own professedly nontheistic, but for me profoundly persuasive and entirely naturalistic, form of religious faith. I make no claim to its absolute truth, but I offer it for rigorous critical reflection and assessment.

Chapter Seven

Religion Without God or Gods

Contrary to the title and theme of philosopher John Dewey's book *A Common Faith*, there is no such thing as a common type of religious faith. Such faith is radically diverse. It has been such throughout human history, and it remains such today. This fact does not call attention to a defect in religion itself, although it has brought about much violence in the history of humans as particular groups of them have tried to force their own distinctive kinds of faith down the throats of others committed to different—sometimes radically different—versions of religious faith. Religion can be a powerful force for good in the world, but it has also proved to be a powerful force for intolerance, conflict, destructiveness, and evil. Intolerance has all too often turned out to be the bane of religion, but it is also testimony to religion's irreplaceable importance in human experience and in the history of human cultures.

The only kind of complete consensus possible in the field of religion is a forced consensus, and that is a contradiction in terms. Different religious traditions and outlooks have a lot to learn from one another, and this is an enterprise well worth supporting. But they also have a lot to learn about the importance and value of recognizing their deep-lying, often irreconcilable differences from and among one another. These differences cannot be eradicated because the issues and problems they speak to are too fundamental and profound to allow for universal persuasion about their possible final resolutions into some kind of unitary, common faith.

The attempt to achieve this outcome is to my mind something like stripping the jewels from each one of a variegated collection of regal diadems in order to reduce their remaining bare frames to a kind of uniformity: one that invites and requires no comparative and disputed aesthetic judgments. A completely consensual form of religious faith would have to be far too simplistic: a bathwater without the baby, a bundle of dry bones without any living sinew or flesh, a bland general formula rather than an intensely personal faith. What makes an ecosystem exciting and alive is its dynamic fluidity and diversity, not a static conformity of its members. Why should it be any different for the field of religion throughout its history and up to the present day?

I do not argue against the need for ongoing constructive dialogue among proponents of different religious traditions that seek not only deeper appreciation and understanding of their differences but also for resolution of at least some of their most contentious differences, wherever possible. At the very least, we should work toward recognizing the great complexity of religious questions and avoiding simplistic, taken-for-granted ways of approaching these questions.

The glory of religious history is to a significant extent its diversity through the ages because this diversity testifies to the multiplicity of issues—intellectual and emotional, historical and social, theoretical and practical—to which it speaks. There may be no addressing all of these issues with equal effectiveness and weight by any one religious tradition. Each will always have much to learn from the others. Each has much to offer to the others. Finally, each religious person has much to learn from other religious persons, and all present religious traditions have much to learn from continuing cultural contributions and changes, particularly those in the natural and social sciences but also in fields such as philosophy and the fine arts.

There is no such thing as absolute, unsurpassable religious truth. Religions must rid themselves of their assumed ability to give final expression to it. We cannot know what the future might bring in ways of deeper, more comprehensive religious conviction. We must live together religiously with open-hearted hope for mutual understanding, and we must avoid at all costs arrogant insistence on one religious outlook at the costs of all others. Adamant demand for some kind of bland, unquestioning religious uniformity is the insidious enemy of personal and communal religious integrity.

What philosopher William James called the ever-mysterious, finally unreachable "More" sought for, spoken of, and pointed to in all forms of religious faith accounts for the irreducible, ever-striving diversity of these forms—a diversity to which his appropriately entitled book *The Varieties of Religious Experience* famously points (1929, 497–501). There may be a common nucleus of problems and concerns faced up to in religious traditions, as James avers, and this would account for our referring to them all as *religious*. But there is no consensus on the appropriate religious responses to these problems and concerns. The diversity of religious traditions and forms of religious faith is not a defect of religion but a reminder of its singular importance in the lives of human beings throughout their history.

With these comments and caveats in mind, I can now proceed to trace some outlines of the type of religious faith I find to be most convincing and transformative. I have referred elsewhere to this faith as *a religion of nature* or as a type of *religious naturalism* (Crosby 2002, 2015). I offer it as a humble participant in ongoing religious dialogue. Who am I to do so? I do so as part of the responsibility implicit in my lifetime vocation as a religious philosopher. But most fundamentally, I write these words as meditations on the religious dimension of human life and on conclusions I have drawn concerning its elusive mysteries and demands over the years of my own life. I make no claim to finality or closure regarding the issues raised, and I would be foolish to do so. The meditations I offer here are tentative and suggestive at best.

I offer these meditations with welcome awareness of my sharing many fundamental ideas about religion with esteemed contemporary religious naturalists such as Connie Barlow, Robert S. Corrington, Ursula Goodenough, Michael S. Hogue, Stuart A. Kauffman, Jea Sophia Oh, Karl E. Peters, Chet Raymo, Loyal Rue, Jerome A. Stone, and Carol Wayne White. We may not agree on everything, of course, but what we do agree on marks us as representatives of an important movement in contemporary religious thought—one well worth articulating to the best of our ability. Its focus on the religious ultimacy of *nature* instead of on the assumed religious ultimacy of a supernatural *God* merits serious consideration in our time of ominous global warming and ecological devastation. Both of these current ecological perils relate intimately to our human attitudes—including, most emphatically, our religious ones—toward nature.

I turn my attention, therefore, away from the professions and defenses of *God's* existence and nature, purpose and will, thought by monotheists such as the ones whose views I discussed in earlier chapters to lie at the heart of authentic religious faith; I shall devote my discussion henceforth to explaining and making a case for the religious ultimacy of *nature*. My central contention is that such a move is not a falling away from authentic religious faith in our time but giving serious consideration to another way to conceive and express such faith that has much to commend it. I write, not in the spirit of proselytizing, but of sharing a form of religious faith that has become deeply meaningful to me over the years of my life.

I shall discuss the following themes in this chapter: the nature of nature, what is religious about nature, the ambiguities of nature, the primal sin in a religion of nature, nature's impersonal character, and the absence of absolute assurance in a religion of nature.

The Nature of Nature

The term *nature* has three fundamental meanings. It can mean either a distinctive characteristic of something, the presently existing cosmos or world, or all possibly existent cosmos or worlds. As for the first meaning, we can say, for example, that it is in the nature of copper to conduct electricity and of rubber to resist it, that it is John's nature to love mathematics and Mary's to be fascinated with biochemistry, that it is in the nature of the democratic system of the United States to allow for and encourage universal human suffrage, and so on. The second usage of the term *nature* is to construe it as referring to the world within which we live, the immense universe—or, more properly, pluriverse—of which we humans are presently a part. And the third usage is to refer to all possible pluriverses—past, present, and future in everlasting time—namely, to the endless series of pluriverses of which ours is but one sequential member.

The first usage will be implicit in what I say about some of the descriptive or characteristic traits of the natural world in which we live. The second usage reminds us of the immensity and complexity of this surrounding world. The third usage guards against the illusion of any creation of something out of nothing and reminds us that all creation is evolution or transformation of one thing out of another. If the present pluriverse has an origin, as contemporary science argues it to have, then it was probably a transformation of the remnants of a previous one, and so on, back into endless time.

So, not only is the present pluriverse enormous beyond our imagining in both space and time, but it also has its own ancient origin in prior pluriverses, back into time with no absolute beginning. Through it all, two and only two primordial principles prevail: *matter-energy* undergoing the evolutionary transformations of endless time, with *time's* unfailing combinations of varying degrees of continuity and novelty, creativity and destructiveness.

Why do I speak of a *pluriverse* rather than of a *universe* when I am describing the nature of nature as I conceive it? For three reasons. The first is that I do not regard nature as some kind of enormous container of its presumed parts. The second reason is that nature is not a static but an intensely dynamic arrangement and interaction of systems within systems, orders within orders, coming into being and passing out of being—something more in the order of a jumble of systems, orders, and feedback relationships, no one of which contains or can contain all of the others. What, precisely then, is nature? It is nothing, in the third place, we can even begin easily to imagine or adequately describe. But at least we can do some justice to it as we experience, study, and relate to it here on earth and in earth's more immediate environs.

Our particle accelerators, radio and light telescopes, cosmic ray detectors, spaceships, and other technical devices, as well as the fertile mathematical and empirical wizardry of our scientists, help to extend our knowledge and awareness far beyond the range of our little solar system. Our present understanding of the nature of nature is fallible, limited, and subject to change. But it gives us much insight into the enormity and complexity of the innumerable orders of nature of which we humans, the earth and its ecosystems, and everything else within our present ken are a part.

All of our descriptions and explanations about nature need assume nothing beyond or outside of nature. We need not endeavor to explain nature but only to explain by means of or in terms of aspects of nature itself. All descriptions and explanations must presuppose something given rather than derived and thus to serve as the basis of such explanations. It would be illogical to try to explain the putative basis or bases of such explanations. If God, for example, were thought to be the creator and sustainer of everything in nature, as monotheists believe, then it would make no sense to ask them to explain how it is possible for God to exist. *God just is*, and everything else *follows*, is one way to understand the traditional monotheistic insistence that God exists necessarily or could not not-be.

In similar fashion, I assume that nature in some mode or manifestation always has been and always will be. There has been no absolute beginning of nature and there will be no absolute end of it, although particular kinds of pluriverses, such as the one of which we humans are presently a part, come into being and pass out of being in endless time. All such pluriverses have been, are now, and forever will be *natural*; this is how I conceive of nature, meaning that nature is *metaphysically ultimate*. All that has existed, exists, or will exist is natural or a manifestation of nature. In other words, nature is all that there is, ever has been, or ever will be.

This is a debatable thesis, to be sure, but it is the one to which I adhere. Its virtue is that it refrains from positing as a basis of explanation for nature itself something outside the range of anything natural or experienceable as such—something I regard as being in the final analysis merely posited, penciled-in, or ad hoc. That something, when regarded as God, is more often than not given attributes that are far beyond the range of comprehensibility, as Feuerbach has argued and as I have strongly been inclined to agree. In my judgment, the basis of a credible explanation should not be even more incredible or unintelligible than what it purports to explain. The supposed omni-attributes of God are a case in point.

What Is Religious About Nature

But is nature an appropriate focus of religious commitment and concern? Does authentic, adequate, meaningful religion not require engagement with something *supernatural,* something greater, more powerful, more personal, caring, and loving than nature by itself could ever be? Apart from creation by, sustenance of, and something like the human face of a personal God, nature seems stern, cold, and indifferent, or so the monotheists we have studied to this point are bound to protest.

Moreover, even if nature in some guise has always existed and will forever continue to exist, it exhibits throughout all of the phases of its changes and developments the deficiencies, limitations, and restrictions of its pervasive *finitude.* It can offer none of the absolute power, promise, and assurance of an infinite, unrestricted, all-powerful God. It lacks, moreover, a comprehensive explanation and purpose for its own being that could be conferred on it only by a purposeful God—or so the argument would run. Without that, nature is soulless and indifferent, no more concerned with us humans than with the rocky face of a mountainside, a subterranean disturbance, or the fleeting, fluttering life of a butterfly.

There is, however, another side of this coin of the religious significance of nature regarded without God or Gods of any kind. There is the everlasting enormity, magnificence, and splendor of nature in its own right. There is its awesome beauty, wondrous complexity, and overpowering majesty. There is, at least here on earth, and in all probability elsewhere in the present pluriverse, the plentiful gift of life in all of its manifold, fascinating forms, including our human form. There is the fact that life is routinely upheld in myriad ways on the face of the earth and that these myriad ways are marvelously interconnected and interdependent with one another. There is so much about nature that takes our breath away if we but take a few moments to contemplate it.

Nature in all of its complexity and diversity is our ground of being. It may have no purpose for its being that we are able confidently to discover, but it is presently replete with purposive beings of innumerable kinds, that is, every kind of life intent on finding ways to adapt to its environment, flourish in that environment, and produce its progeny to continue doing so. Whether or not contemporary nature has some antecedent, comprehensive, special purpose for its being, it is full of inherent purposes and purposive activities of many different kinds, including the purposive activities of our human lives. Causal determinists may deny that there are such things as purposes freely arrived at, purposively entertained, striven toward, and enacted; however, such denial cannot help but presuppose that there are such, if the denial and arguments given in its support are to be responded to as being themselves believable, purposeful, intentional, and free actions.

Religious people often yearn for *miracles* to vouchsafe the truth of their religious traditions. But nature overflows with miracles or wonders of countless kinds, miracles so routine and commonplace as to be generally taken for granted and overlooked—and only brought to our jaded attention by the eye of the artist, the skill of the poet, the talent of the musician, the searching questions of the philosopher, or the contemplations of deeply sensitive religious persons. A miracle need not be some kind of interruption of the laws of nature. It can more likely be regarded as the many different exhibitions of the regularities of nature—the rumble of thunder; a twisting flash of lightning; the birth of a child; the restoration of a habitat after a devastating flood, landslide, or fire; the steadily pulsating life in our own breast during our lifetimes; the gift of life in all of its countless nonhuman forms; and the incalculable gift of love, whenever and however it is expressed or bestowed.

Nature may not love us in the ways other humans or other types of sentient creatures can, but it enables us to love one another as humans and actively to love and ardently give thanks for our interdependent relations as humans with the whole gamut of living beings on the face of the earth. Nature is not some kind of distinctive being in the way that a personal God is thought by monotheists to be. It is the whole range of beings—living and nonliving—and the manifold systems and orders that enable them to function, interrelate, and be.

Ambiguities of Nature

What, then, of all of the ambiguities, uncertainties, threats, and undependable aspects of nature, its indissoluble blend of joys and sufferings, creations and destructions, the expected and the unexpected, and the like? What about its plagues, wildfires, earthquakes, tsunamis, hurricanes, tornadoes, and floods? What about the predatory preying of life on life and the bitter mourning for life's all-too-frequent premature deaths? What about the fact of inevitable death itself? These facts seem to stand in stark contrast with the will and purpose of a loving, dependable, perfect God and seem hardly to qualify nature itself as an appropriate focus of religious faith.

But this contrast conveniently leaves out of account the monotheistic conviction that God has created the world and continues to order and sustain its existence. If the ambiguities of nature are a problem for the religious naturalist, they are much more so for the monotheist who sees them as aspects of nature that are purposefully created and intended as such by God.

There are at least two ways in which monotheists could respond to this kind of question. One is that if God is to create anything other than God, then it would have to be finite and less than perfect. The second way is that of the apostle Paul and the later Christian Church, namely, that the dread uncertainties and imperfections of the present world, in all its nonhuman as well as human aspects, are consequences of the sinfulness of God's human creatures. With their primordial fall into sin and disobedience to God—or so the argument goes—the whole world fell into corruption and disarray. We human creatures were evicted from paradise and forced to live in the present radically ambiguous, corrupt, imperfect, and hazardous world.

A time in the future will come for the world's complete reformation and redemption, but we must now await the coming of that time with anxious, poignant longing and trusting faith (see Romans 8: 18–22). We can see today that there is some truth to this picture of nature radically endangered by rampant, heedless human technological exploitation and misuse: a picture made credible by the current ecological crisis on earth that is being brought about to a large and increasingly alarming extent by human beings. But this is a local, earthly phenomenon, not one of cosmic proportions.

Primal Sin in a Religion of Nature

There is something like a primal sin in a religion of nature, and human sinfulness itself is no stranger to it. There are at least three aspects of this primal sin: seeing ourselves as lords of nature rather than as humble participants in its community of living beings on earth; a tragic lack of empathy for other life forms, for their wants, sufferings, and needs; and a deeply regrettable sense of despair by humans with regard to their finite human condition—in other words, with respect to their being creatures of nature here on earth. For a religion of nature there is no entitlement for humans to dominate nature, preside over it, stand outside it, or subject it endlessly and unrestrictedly to human wants, needs, desires, or uses.

We are not created in the image of a God but in the image of nature, part and parcel of its bone and flesh. As such, we can be humble participants in its processes along with all of the other life forms on earth. We are part of a democracy of creatures, not masters at the peak of an aristocratic hierarchy. We have special gifts, to be sure, but misuse of these gifts—as in our pervasive, uncaring fossil-fuel technology and in our heedless, selfish overrunning of natural habitats—can bring, and is bringing on all sides, disaster and ruin, not only to ourselves but to much of the earth's natural biosphere. Our prideful self-centeredness is a sin of enormous magnitude and reach, and of woefully destructive consequences.

The second aspect of the primal sin brought into focus by a religion of nature is the large-scale absence of empathy for the other life forms of earth that is now and has long been typical of human beings. We have strong, unthinking tendency to view other kinds of life as mere means to our human ends or as obstructions to those ends. We have viewed them as manipular objects or mere *things* rather than living *subjects* akin in many respects to our own modes of being. We have shown indifference toward their sufferings and toward the aspirations and needs distinctive to their individual forms of life. We do not stop to think what their lives are for them, thinking only of how they can be managed and put to use by us. They are nothing more, at best, than brute "resources."

Religion of nature counsels us to be constantly and appreciatively aware that we are surrounded by life forms other than our own throughout the earth, and that we should respect and honor those forms as sacred. Failure to do so, as we so typically have in the past, is a primal sin, the seed of untold suffering for all of life on earth. Empathy for other life forms is not some kind of poetic garnish on the real issues of human existence. It lies at the heart of what it means to be a responsible and viable citizen among the earth's creatures.

Christianity has long entreated us to love our neighbors as we love ourselves. But who is our neighbor? Religion of nature's answer to this searching question is that every kind of life on the face of the earth is our neighbor, our closely related evolutionary and ecological kith and kin. And we had best soon come to love them every bit as much as we have loved ourselves as humans. But how do I love, care for, and properly relate to a tree, a shrub, a racoon, a hog, a chicken, a cow, a honeybee, a trout, a frog, a salamander? We had better soon find out, or we invite ruin on them as well as on ourselves.

Finally, there is the primordial sin of despair in response to the finitude of human life here on earth. We still seem to be guilty at bottom of the temptation of Eve in the Garden: "You shall be like God" if you but eat of the fruit of this tree (Genesis 3: 5). We are not at all satisfied with or grateful for being humans; we want ourselves and our human loved ones to be like the supposed angels with God in heaven—forever perfect, forever at rest, with none of the restrictions, hazards, difficulties, and demands of finite human existence. We scorn the gift of our finite lives on earth. We feel that life is pointless if it must end in the alleged pointlessness of our deaths. We ache with yearning to be or to become something we are not.

Nature generously bestows life on us and we unthankfully reject it. If nature is all that there is, and we are nothing more than one of its creatures, then we succumb to a mood of desperation and despair. This seems in a telling way to be the attitude of many *monotheists* as they contemplate our lives as humans on earth. Nature is not enough! We must have much more! Otherwise, our lives are ultimately pointless and absurd.

All of this way of thinking is for a religion of nature the way of sinful ingratitude and faithless rejection of the gift of life. It implies a haughty indifference to the well-being of nature itself that can have disastrous consequences for humans and for many of the other creatures of the earth. *To be is to be finite*; we humans are not exemptions to this natural rule. We should give thanks for this rule rather than rejecting it out of hand because it is a necessary concomitant of our being conscious and alive. And it supplies us with gifts and capabilities that enable us to be of use in the world. Nature in any particular form of a given pluriverse may not last forever, as I believe to be the case. But all of its cosmic products through endless time are finite, as are each of its successive forms of manifestation such as that of our own natural world. Is any sequential pluriverse less bountiful or wonderful for all of that? Is finitude itself a fatal flaw?

To reject our character as creatures of nature because of despair over our finitude seems to me like the spoiled son who rejects his father's generous birthday gift of a beautiful new automobile because it is not of the color the son would have preferred, because its power or speed is limited, or even more absurdly, because the son knows that the magnificent automobile will someday wear out and will not and cannot function forever. No human life is perfect. None will last forever on the face of this earth. But all are sacred and precious in their potentiality for exemplary self-realization and service to one another, if not always in their conscious and intentional attainments. Each of us is in need of others, as well as our having the capability of using our finite resources in helpfulness to others. Those finite human resources are also desperately needed today in service for the well-being of a grievously endangered planet earth and its countless nonhuman inhabitants.

Nature's gift of finite life to us humans should not be thoughtlessly and thanklessly taken for granted, deplored, or rejected. The long-held conviction that our lives here on earth are temporary launching pads for our true home in heaven should itself, in my opinion as proponent of a religion of nature, be rejected as implicitly wrongheaded and even destructively so, as it takes vital attention away from our gifts and responsibilities as integral parts of nature. We are finite; our contributions are finite; everything around us is finite; even this present cosmos or face of nature is finite.

But the majesty, glory, and wonder of this present pluriverse and of our natural home is not in the least marred or diminished by its finitude. Finitude is the irremediable way of being something, not an ineradicable defect. Finitude brings its injustices, its tragedies, its evils, its sufferings, its ever-present dangers. These are also risks of finite freedom. But finite nature also confers its gifts of life and its prospects of accomplishment and joy for most, even if sadly not for all.

There is an undeniably tragic aspect about nature and of life in nature. This fact reflects its finitude. But its finitude also makes possible its satisfactions and fulfillments. Either we reject all existence on account of its intractable ambiguities, or we accept and make the most of those ambiguities as best we can. In my view as a religious naturalist, there is no other choice. Humble thankfulness and helpfulness, laced with compassionate, empathetic sadness is our only viable way of life.

This is admittedly easy enough for the relatively fortunate ones among us to say, and it may be extremely difficult for the less fortunate to acknowledge. But we can at least try to work together for as much common justice, healthiness, long life, meaningful work, and goodness as is possible for us to bring about for others in the finite conditions of our lives on earth. Finitude is not some kind of primordial, avoidable defect or consequence of sin for the religious naturalist. To think of it in this way and to pine for some imagined infinite, allegedly perfect kind of existence is a misperception and misplacing of what is possible or even conceivable for creatures like us—many theologians "to the contrary notwithstanding," as the familiar saying goes.

Here I register a fundamental disagreement with those who see the hope of heaven and the putative perfections of God and of God's heaven as necessary deliverance from the imperfections, tragedies, risks, and inequalities of finite life on earth. Tillich is surely right to stress *coping* with finitude as the important and even central challenge of all relevant kinds of religious faith, but it would be a serious mistake, in my humble judgment, to think that religion can promise any meaningful way to *eliminate* it. For me, as I have emphasized, to be is to be natural, and to be natural is to be finite. This statement applies to all of the faces of nature throughout endless time, and to all of its orders and constituents therein. As far as I am able to discern, nature in some shape or form is all that there is now, ever has been, or ever will be. *And the natural is enough.*[1]

However, for the monotheist the natural is not enough and can never be enough. Why? Because nature is impersonal. It is not a conscious being. It cannot love us, care for us, or cherish our human situation in any kind of helpful manner. Nature is blank, blind, and unfeeling, no less so than any kind of artifact or machine. My house does not care for me and neither does my refrigerator. Rocks do not concern themselves with my well-being any more than the mosquito thrusting its hungry proboscis into my upper arm on a hot summer day.

In this perspective, nature is cold and indifferent, as likely to wipe out me and all that I cherish at any moment, as it is to support my life and all that I care for and love. Nature is not my conscious enemy, of course, but neither is it, nor can it be, my conscious friend. Since nature cannot save us or respond to our deepest religious aspirations and needs, a so-called religion of nature is a misnomer. Only God, as the personal, conscious creator and sustainer of nature and everything within it—including us humans—can play this much-needed role in our lives as humans. But our human bodies are part of nature, and they critically rely on other parts of nature such as food and water, materials out of which to build shelter, a breathable atmosphere, and places to live. These necessities are not always forthcoming from nature alone. The same is true of a healthy, well-functioning human body.

This critical monotheistic response to a religion of nature is guilty of a fundamental confusion, in my view. It thinks of nature as some kind of grand abstraction rather than recognizing its many layers of complex reality. Nature as an abstraction does of course not think, recognize, care, or feel about anything, including itself. It has no basis beyond itself for all of the complex forms of life it has produced and continues to produce. But it is full of sentient beings who can experience and feel, consider and evaluate, interpret and understand—to varying degrees of attunement, competence, and attainment.

We humans can have countless versions of what Martin Buber famously has called "I-Thou" relationships, with one another and with other sentient creatures of nature—especially with those whose degrees of sentient awareness approach our own. Aspects of nature have brought us humans into being and sustain us in being as long as we live. They have conferred on us the gifts of life, aspiration, hope, challenge, purpose, value, and meaning. They impart to us courage to live with gratitude as well as compassionate care for the gift of our finite existence and in response to the challenges it places before us to be of help to one another and to all of the other creatures of the earth. *Our finitude is not just restriction and limitation; it is also capacity and enablement.* It is important that we develop our ability to view it and put it into use in this manner.

We do so as natural beings and in ways similar to those of all other natural beings. And we do so within a finite span of life, along with all the other life forms of the earth. We may at times be tempted to deplore our finitude and indulge in wishes for an endless, so-called perfect life. But this is a futile and pointless dream, and it is far from clear how satisfying or fulfilling it would actually turn out to be if were somehow to become possible or be realized.

In short, awareness of finitude need not imply pointlessness and despair. It can be recognized for what it offers in the ways of aspiration and attainment, but also with full acknowledgment of what it fails to provide for those whose lives are stricken with inordinate amounts of tragedy and suffering, and whose lives cry out for the compassionate care and concern by the more fortunate among us. Above all else, we are called upon to recognize and work against those systemic factors in our social and cultural institutions that permit or cause needless deprivation and suffering, either for us humans or for any individuals or groups of the nonhuman sentient beings of nature.[2] Our finite condition, far from being some sort of hopelessly tragic dead end, can give us empathy, motivation, means, and capability to do so on behalf of others. Finitude is admittedly a mixed blessing, but a blessing, nonetheless. It calls out for caring compassion and love toward one another and all other living beings in a way that infinite perfection never could.

No Absolute Assurance in a Religion of Nature

But unlike the traditional God of monotheistic religion, monotheistic theologians are likely to argue, religion of nature provides no assurance of the ultimate triumph of goodness over evil. Without such assurance, it is not even clear how it can rightly be called a type of religion. There is, for example, no vision of the promised return of Jesus the Christ in glory, no sure establishment of the Kingdom of God or of a new heaven and a new earth: in short, no guaranteed eschatological hope. An infinitely powerful and flawlessly good God can guarantee the fulfillment of such hope in a way that finite nature does not and cannot.

But there is a fly in the ointment of this alleged guarantee. That fly is *human freedom.* Absolute assurance of the final triumph of goodness over evil requires an overruling of the contingency of freedom, of its capability of choosing the evil over the good to the point of bringing ultimate destruction to the earth itself or at least the end of human civilization—or even the human species—on the earth. Monotheists have typically argued that God bestows on human beings the inestimable gift and responsibility of freedom. God does so because God is a God of love who yearns for a relationship of love with God's human creatures. One cannot be in love with a robot; genuine love requires the free response of the beloved and can be satisfied with nothing less.

In creating us free, God takes the unavoidable risk of our ultimate human betrayal and rejection of the gift of divine love and its necessary gift of freedom. Eschatological *hope*, therefore, is different from eschatological *guarantee* in monotheistic religion—even though this fact is all too often overlooked there. There is no escape from the finitude, contingency, and the uncertain future of genuine human freedom, *not even for God.* God must have hope for and faith in the free gift of love God bestows on us, even as we must have faith in God's promised steadfast free love for us.

The triumph of goodness is the triumph of love, whether it be love for God or love for our fellow humans, for the other living beings of nature, and for nature itself as our true home. As free beings, we are charged with the responsibility of bringing as much goodness into the world as is possible for us. This is our gift of love to one another and to the natural world we inhabit. There cannot be genuine love without genuine freedom, and genuine freedom offers reliable hope but no absolute guarantees. Religion of nature is as much a religion of love and loving hope as any kind of monotheism.

There is no escape from the risks and uncertainties of the future, for us, for God—if there be a God—or for a nature that produces and permits such a thing as free beings such as ourselves. A God exercising total control of the future cannot be a God of love. The enhancement of freedom so necessary for love is also the enhancement of risk and uncertainty.

Paradoxically, the surety of salvation, whether in monotheistic religion, religion of nature, or any other kind of religion, depends crucially on the risks and grave responsibilities of human freedom. Nature as the ground of our being confers freedom upon us and continuously relies on its responsible use from us on our severely threatened planet. It strengthens our hand in myriad ways even as it is itself in dire need of the strength of our wholly natural human hand. We are co-creators and co-sustainers of the natural orders here on earth.

I argue that nature needs us humans for continuation of its present forms of life on earth as much as we need it. This is religious gift and responsibility of the highest order and most profound significance. There is nothing trivial, superficial, or sentimental about a religion of nature. And, I continue to argue, nothing is incomplete or lacking in nature as far as living with confident, richly meaningful, religious faith is concerned.

Conclusion

This chapter has defended a religion of nature against some of the most prevalent criticisms monotheists are likely to direct against it. I have sought to make the case for monotheistic religion itself as subtle, far-ranging, and convincing as I can by critically examining the thoughtful arguments presented on its behalf by some influential monotheists of the nineteenth and twentieth centuries, and up to the present—most of them Christian, but one of them an exemplary Jewish thinker. I have then contrasted these arguments for monotheism with relevant arguments on behalf of a religion of nature, at least as I conceive some of the major features of the latter.

In the process of this investigation, I have also tried to bring into focus some of the commonalities of conviction and concern that are implicit in the two perspectives. These overlap in some significant ways even as they differ significantly in others. Each deserves to be honored and respected as examples of the age-old search for religious meaning, truth, and transformation. A dialogue of monotheism and naturalism such as the one I have set up here can bring out some fundamental differences in the two religious outlooks, but it should not be allowed to obscure the fundamental similarities of function, question, analysis, and argument that also underlie them. I hope to have made this point clear as the book has progressed.

I included Ludwig Feuerbach in my discussion because I think that he takes accurate aim at a central aspect of monotheism: namely, its latent anthropocentricism and its all too explicit privileging and radical separating of human beings from the other creatures of nature. Such thinking runs abruptly and cross-purposively against the grain of all that we know today about biological evolution. It is the telling symptom of thinking that is outmoded and out of alignment with our present ways of regarding the world and our place as humans within it.

This is not to say that all that is assumed to be known in the present is undoubtedly true and that everything in the past is obviously wrong. It is only to say that what we receive from the past is not necessarily—in virtue of that fact alone—true, and that it may require reinterpretation and openness to newer, more adequate ways of thinking. Such critical thinking should not leave out of account features of traditional monotheism that reflect the possibly outmoded thought patterns of earlier times.

It is especially high time for us to move away from the features of an older, now increasingly obsolete way of thinking about nature and the place of humans in nature. We are in desperate need now to *decenter* human beings and their long-held claim to mirror the awesome character of a supernatural God and to belong fundamentally to another supernatural, purely spiritual world—and to *recenter* nature itself as the welcome ground, milieu, and home of our human lives.

This is a milieu overflowing with innumerable lives of different kinds, all of them exhibiting in many ways remarkable similarities to the aspirations, needs, and situations of our own species. They are neighbors we should strive to love and care for, even as we humans instinctively love and care for ourselves. We are truly at home here and not in some other imagined world. These are central theses of a religion of nature, and all else in our finite, wholly natural human lives depends on and flows from them. To have the high honor, privilege, and responsibility of being a creature of nature is no less evocative and wondrous than to be regarded as a creature of God. Nor is it in any way less demanding and saving in its willing acknowledgment of the opportunities, responsibilities, and limits of a finite and irreversibly mortal human life.

I firmly agree with Martin Buber's insistence on the fundamental importance of intimate relationships and especially with the ground of our being. But that relationship is with nature in my view, not with God. We owe to nature the fealty, commitment, trust, devotion, compassion, and love monotheists center on God. God is remote and austere, disembodied and purely spiritual, unlike, in God's essential being, anything in this world. God deigns to care for us humans but has no real need for us, having an inviolable self-sufficiency. God preexisted nature and would continue to exist were nature to pass out of being. The gap between nature and God as traditionally conceived seems unbridgeable in principle, whereas there is no gap between us as natural beings and the nature of which we are an intimate part. Our home is here, and our duties and responsibilities are here. We are destined to live and die here, along with all of the innumerable other creatures of nature.

But while we are here, we have essential roles to play. Other aspects of life on earth are crucially dependent on our accepting and carrying out these roles faithfully. The meaning of our human lives lies in our relations as creatures gifted by evolution with extraordinary capabilities to put those special capabilities to use in being good and effective servants of nature, not in arrogantly and futilely trying to dominate and bend nature to our selfish wills. Our empathy, compassion, and love can be extended to all forms of life on earth rather than being restricted to our own species and to something suspiciously like ourselves but raised to an extraordinary degree and given the name of God. For a religious naturalist like me, nature has a deeply spiritual character and inexhaustible sacred allure despite its being physical and embodied, through and through. The physical and the spiritual, far from being alien to one another, are one and the same. The spiritual indwells the physical, and the physical sustains it in being.

But is nature really so sacred and fitting a focus of religious faith as I have claimed in this chapter and elsewhere in this book? Is faith in it really comparable to faith in God? I find convincing testimony to this effect in the words of novelist Vladimir Nabokov, as in 1948 he reminisced on his experiences as a boy and later as a man fascinated by the many species of butterflies. "To stand among rare butterflies and their food plants," he proclaims, is something he cannot venture to explain, something "like a momentary vacuum into which rushes all that I love, a sense of oneness with sun and stone, a thrill of gratitude to whom it may concern, perhaps to the contrapuntal genius of human fate or to the tender ghosts humoring a lucky mortal." Here is wonder, mystery, miracle, and ecstasy of the highest order. It is even, he suggests an experience of "the highest enjoyment of timelessness" (Nabokov 2023, 19). No more needs to be said by any who have had similar experiences. This is *religious experience* in its purest, most explicit form, and its focus is squarely on nature itself, not on God. Nabokov was anxious to capture new species of butterflies for his collection. I am content to watch them go about their business as I go about mine.

The experience Nabokov so tenderly describes took place among the lupines, columbines, penstemons, and Mariposa lilies in the vicinity of Longs Peak in northern Colorado. I lived not far from that extremely high mountain and even climbed to its flat, spacious top on one occasion. I spent many a day hiking among the same flowers Nabokov mentions and glorying in the mountains awesomely rising above me and beckoning my ascent. On one day I especially remember, I climbed almost vertically aside a waterfall and emerged finally atop its ridge. There lay suddenly before my gaze from that vantage point a lovely tarn, and beyond it, ranges of snow-capped peaks stretching into the distance. I still vividly remember my shock and delight in coming upon this enchanting vision of the wonders of nature. Here is revelation of an especially revealing and deeply inspiring kind.

To tread on this marvelous earth is to tread on sacred ground, an inestimable privilege, not for a moment to be scorned or simply taken for granted. The same is true of soaring above the cloud-speckled earth in airplanes or spaceships, or probing the darkening depths of its oceans and seas. Everywhere there is life, tumultuous, teeming life—on the earth, beneath its surface, submerged in its waters, and aloft in its air—and we are remarkably privileged to live among countless living beings of many other kinds than we humans.

There is oxygen for respiration in ocean and air, and there is carbon dioxide for the photosynthesis of plants. We need to work tirelessly to keep the two in proper balance, and not to destroy that delicate balance with the harsh intrusions of our fossil fuels. We need to respect and uphold the lives of other creatures on earth and to be profoundly aware of the ever-present danger of their extinctions. We have no need for another home or the promise of another way of life beyond our graves.

There is opportunity enough, challenge enough, and fulfilment enough here—enough to last each of us a lifetime and to require of our human institutions and communities the highest possible levels of awareness and effort, discernment and responsibility. Nature has much to teach us, and we have much to learn. We are not its masters but its humble and, in many ways, seriously flawed servants. We can and must do better—to tirelessly work to renovate, refresh, and renew, instead of thoughtlessly to ravage, wreck, and destroy our natural home and the fragile lives of its nonhuman inhabitants.

Chapter Eight

Physics, Biology, and a Philosophical Perspective on Religious Naturalism

We saw in chapter 5 how the physicist John Polkinghorne reasoned from his experience as a quantum physicist that the existence of a personal God is required to make sense of the existence of the world. And we noted how central to his reasoning was the *cosmological anthropic principle*, namely, that there is sufficient complexity, order, temporal open-endedness, and fine-tuning in our world to allow for the evolution of human beings. This, he contended, could not simply be accidental. It had to be purposeful and intended. The world was intended to be this way by a purposeful God. God created human beings as conscious free agents so that God could invite them into loving relationships with their creator and with one another.

Notable in this reasoning is not only the *centrality of God* as a distinctive, existent being, but also the assumed *centrality of humans*, and perhaps other creatures similar to them elsewhere in the whole of nature. Cosmic, terrestrial, and biological evolution was intended by God to produce us humans on earth as its overarching goal. Quantum physics was recently discovered in physics as its necessary basis, allowing for the workings of chance, and biological evolution—drawing on this basis—reached its divinely intended goal in the evolution of humans. There may be beings similar to humans elsewhere in the cosmos, but presumably the same kind of reasoning would explain their evolution and subsequent existence as well.

In other words, it would all seem for Polkinghorne to be ultimately about *God and us*, and creatures similar in critical respects to us (if any), elsewhere in the cosmos. Everything else about our present far-flung cosmos is finally explained by Polkinghorne, theoretical physicist and Anglican priest, in this manner. Ludwig Feuerbach would have been delighted with this seeming confirmation of his central thesis. The *cosmological anthropic principle* is rightly named. Its focus is on *anthropos*, and the idea of God is a colossal magnification of this focus made into the ground or basis of the cosmos as a whole. Attention is taken away, at least implicitly, from the rest of nature and placed on us humans and an all-too-human-like personal God. Chet Raymo is *another physicist* who, in contrast to the thought of Polkinghorne, takes strong issue with this way of interpreting the world.

The Religious Naturalism of Physicist Chet Raymo

Raymo earned a doctoral degree in physics from the University of Notre Dame and spent much of his adult life teaching physics at Stonehill College in northeastern Massachusetts. Although reared in Roman Catholicism and studying and teaching at Roman Catholic institutions of higher education, he became a convinced religious naturalist. As such, he takes the focus of religion entirely off of us and a humanlike God and places it squarely on what he regards as the ultimacy of nature itself, a nature without God, a nature that is *its own sacred ground*.

"The personhood of God," he writes, "is the memetic offspring of human imagination. So, yes, toss it. But retain the waters of refreshment, the beautiful and terrible mystery that soaks creation as water soaks a rag, diminished by any name we give it—the abiding, intuited, Ultimate X" (Raymo 2008, 103). This terrible mystery of nature is also, for Raymo, the seat of the *sacred*, the *everything in nature*—and not in some faraway *heaven*—that persists and presents itself to religious receptivity and awareness as recognizably *holy*, especially when the monotheistic, personal God is frankly acknowledged to be no longer real (thus the above referenced book's provocative title: *When God Is Gone, Everything Is Holy*, and its instructive subtitle: *The Making of a Religious Naturalist*). Nature in all of its evocative splendor and mystery is for him the rightful focus of ardent, faithful, persistently searching religious commitment and concern.

And nature is far—*extremely far*—from being confined to this earth or to its comparatively miniscule solar system. "Not long ago," Raymo exclaims, "we imagined ourselves to be the be-all and end-all of creation, at the center of a cosmos made expressly for us. We stood at the pinnacle of the material Great Chain of Being, just a step away below the spiritual angels. We could almost touch the hem of God's robe as he sat on his celestial throne in the all-enclosing Empyrean sphere." Then, starting with Copernicus, we discovered that "our star, our planet, the life on it, and even our own intelligence, are completely mediocre" (133–34). Talk about a radical decentering of *anthropos* and, implicitly, of an anthropomorphic *God*! This kind of sobering realization can be the basis for shifting our religious attention away from the earth and a humanlike God to the vastness, mystery, and sacredness of nature.

Raymo therefore claims that "at this moment in history, the most reliable way of knowing the natural world is science," a science that definitely includes his own field of physics (103). There is here no need for appeal to revelations supposedly given to humans by a personal God. And there is no justification for mortal conflict between religion and science such as that claimed by Richard Dawkins. Instead, there is the summons for a deep sensitivity to the religious meaning and saving power of lifelong close attention to the immanent sacredness of nature in all of its aspects, a sensitivity that can and ought continuously to be expanded and enhanced by advances in scientific understanding as well as by innumerable other experiences and endeavors of the questing human spirit. This is religious naturalism in a nutshell, and the physicist Raymo is one of its most devoted, articulate, and persuasive proponents.

Raymo was reared and nourished by Roman Catholicism in his earlier years. And he continues to cherish much of its spirit, ritual, and symbolism. But he no longer accepts its hierarchical authoritarianism or the central place within it of its conception of a radically transcendent and yet somehow preeminently personal God. His abiding sense of the immanent presence, power, and mystery of the *sacred* carries resolutely over, however, into his present faith as a religious naturalist. "Let it only be said," he insists, "that the world is shot through with a mystery that manifests itself no less in what is revealed by science—the universe of the galaxies and the eons, the eternally weaving DNA, the electrochemical flickering that is consciousness—than in the creation of novelist, poets, visual artists, and musicians. So we stumble forward, trying to avoid the dogmas of blind faith or scientism" (126). And "stumble forward" he has, throughout his life, seeking ways to acclimate his own life and to invite others into the sensibilities and searchings of a devoted religious naturalist.

An engaging example of these ways of acclimation and sensitization is set forth in Raymo's beautifully written earlier book *Honey from Stone: A Naturalist's Search for God*. A better subtitle might have been *A Naturalist's Search for the Holy in Nature* because what he finds, particularly in later aspects of his search, is not the personal deity of traditional Christianity but the holy mystery resident in every aspect of nature. Resident, this is to say, for those willing to open their minds and hearts to its sacred presence and to do so with disciplined, sustained, educatable focus and commitment.

Admittedly, it takes more than just a committed spirit to be able to spend eight summers on the Dingle Peninsula of Ireland attuning one's ear to hear the voice of the sacred in nature in a faraway, remote place adjacent to the North Atlantic Ocean. It also takes the free time and the appropriate means for doing so, which Raymo was fortunate to have. But I applaud him for his intense dedication to this task and for the writing of this splendid earlier book. His training in physics taught him the invaluable lesson of close attention to physical details, and that close attention is evident on every page of this remarkable book. The *honey* of its title is the marvel of the sacred he found lurking there in every ancient *stone* formation in Dingle and in its many different forms of life. Fellow religious seekers like me are privileged to read of his wise and inspiring findings from those eight summers. I heartily recommend this book to you, the reader, as well. With a welcoming bid to his Roman Catholic acculturation, the book is arranged under the eight canonical "hours" of the medieval monastery. It is a book of inspired and inspiring religious contemplations, fittingly set within the environs of a seventh-century CE monastic settlement and a still extant twelfth-century stone church that probably replaced an earlier one made of wood (74).

I also recommend Raymo's intriguingly titled book *Natural Prayers* (1999). These are prayers of careful observation, detailed description, and grateful commentary on innumerable aspects of the natural world. Their spirit of fascination with the wonders of nature, and of intense devotion to the sacredness of these wonders, is infectious and inspiring in the highest degree. Raymo's careful observations, beautifully described in this book, range across spiders, dragon flies, dandelions, oysters, jellyfish, frogs, birds, trees, flowers and the like, each observation and description a kind of prayer.

At one point in this marvelous book, he attributes his profound sensibility to the sacredness of nature mainly to his early religious upbringing: "I was raised a Roman Catholic, and something of that faith clings to me like a sweet odor that won't wash away. A sense of mystery. A sense of the sacred and the sacramental. A profound attraction to the symbolic possibilities of earth, air, fire, and water." But he then tellingly confesses, "I have drifted away from the professions of the Creed, yet I retain an indelible affinity for the tradition of creation mysticism that has been strong in the Roman faith" (1999, 115–16). I can say much the same on behalf of my own rearing in the Protestant faith and its versions of "creation mysticism" that are not so different from the Roman Catholic versions or from the ones that breathe through the common scriptures of these two religious faiths.

Raymo's books are the musings of physicist, philosopher, and poet. They contain careful reportage, analysis, and insight. They are especially attuned to the alluring mysteries of the starry night. They speak profoundly to our emotions as well as our intellects. They are *revelatory* in their own fashion, but they speak to minds and hearts willing to take seriously the voice of contemporary science and of an admittedly Godless, and yet intensely holy, all-surrounding nature—*the nature that is its own ground.*

There is no purposeful, conscious, presiding Deity here, but there is limitless power to motivate, empower, orient, and inspire. Raymo's writings open to our gaze to the kindly but also often mysterious and flickering light of nature's leading. They help us to acknowledge and come to terms with the sometimes harsh, abrupt threats, tragedies, and uncertainties of our temporal, limiting, finitude as creatures of nature. The religious path of nature has its arduous aspects, but it also has many calming, welcoming, saving ones as well.

Raymo is an especially gifted purveyor of the latter, but he does not allow the former to be enveloped in an overly sentimental, romantic haze. As creatures of nature, we are no less subject to nature's complexities and obdurate laws than any other natural being. And those laws do not focus exclusively on us, nor do they originate from the intentional actions of a humanlike, personal God. As a well-educated physicist, university professor, and lifelong student of nature, Raymo does not doubt that this is and must be true. He presents a convincing case for his conviction and commitment as a religious naturalist.[1]

The Religious Naturalism of
Biologist Stuart A. Kauffman

The second religious naturalist I want to discuss in this final chapter is the theoretical biologist Stuart A. Kauffman, who defends his religious outlook in a book tellingly entitled *Reinventing the Sacred: A New View of Science, Reason, and Religion.* I include him in the present book partly for the provocative way in which he brings his interpretation of biological science into discussion as a substantial contributor, rather than as a stubborn barrier, to relevant and meaningful religious thought. Raymo views his academic field of physics in similar fashion, as I point out in this chapter, and we saw in chapter 5 how Polkinghorne drew on his expertise as a quantum physicist to defend his monotheistic metaphysics and lifelong religious faith.

Kauffman strongly resists, however, the idea that biology can be reduced to physics or that it is only a subset to physics, as all else in the world is often assumed or claimed by some physicists to be. He is a theoretical foe of reductionism and a champion of the evidences of genuine creativity to be found throughout the realm of biology. Biological creativity certainly includes many aspects of the phenomena described in physics, but it is not reducible to these aspects. Biological evolution is the antithesis of reduction of everything in the cosmos to the constituent, principles, and laws of physics. Its direction is forward, not backward. Kauffman concedes that reductionism sometimes plays an important role in natural science, but he argues that this role is limited rather than all-encompassing. "Biology is really not just physics," he argues. "Nor are organisms nothing but physics. Organisms are parts of the furniture of the universe, with causal powers of their own, that change the actual physical evolution of the universe. Biology is emergent with respect to physics. Life, agency, value, meaning, and consciousness have all emerged in the evolution of the biosphere" (Kauffman 2008, 43).

The operative word in his statement is *emerged* because this word connotes a future-oriented evolutionary and not just a past-oriented, reductionistic perspective—a continuous coming into being of genuine novelty and not just the perturbations of something already complete and antecedently existent. This ongoing biological creativity or evolutionary production of novelty in the world is for Kauffman the fulcrum for his vision of religious naturalism and the principal basis for his hope and challenge of "reinventing of the sacred." The "re" of his title tells it all. His focus throughout is on the dynamism of the emerging *new* and not on the fixity of the already established *old*, that is, on the laws of physics that provided the necessary physical context and basis for the *new* creation of life on earth. But even this context and basis emerged from earlier forms of energy and patterns of emergent enactments stemming from the conjectured "big bang" of current physical theory. Cosmic evolution is complemented by ongoing terrestrial evolution—and that by ongoing biological evolution.

Physics does not describe, nor should it undertake the task of describing, everything that exists in terms of itself. Biology has its own distinctive, irreducible laws, just as physics does. The latter kinds of law not only help to explain the emergence of life, mind, and culture—along with the irreducible, wondrous creativity of each—but also that these biological laws are themselves emergent from, rather than reducible to, the sorts of theoretical discoveries characteristic of the field of physics.

Kauffman is particularly critical of the idea of the causal closedness of the cosmos. He contends that a central feature of biological evolution is increasing degrees and types of genuine autonomy and freedom as organisms of all types work continuously to adapt successfully to their ecological environments, and often even change those environments in important ways. Such freedom is an outcome of evolutionary processes, but it also gives to the creatures of those evolutionary processes the emergent freedom of autonomous, discerning, resourceful modes of creative adaptation to, and transformative use of, aspects of their natural environments.

Kauffman is no theoretical friend of the kind of mind-body dualism endorsed by the theologian Richard Swinburne and implicit in much Christian thinking about a purely spiritual heaven with its purely spiritual angels, God, and humans taken as spiritual substances out of their old bodies in order to reside everlastingly in that heaven. Most fundamentally for our purposes, Kauffman is a thoroughgoing naturalist—and a *religious* naturalist to boot. He has no sympathy for anything claimed to be supernatural.

The focus of his religious naturalism is not just what the medieval thinkers called *natura naturata*, or the present face of nature, but much more resolutely on what they also referred to as *natura naturans*, nature's ongoing creative processes, changes, surprises, and new developments. Kauffman's nature is a nature with a constant orientation to the future rather than one fixed interminably on a causally determined present and past. It is a pervasively dynamic system, not a static one or one reducible to fixed causes or to endlessly routine, unchanging processes and laws.

If creativity, rather than mere repetition and conformity, is the key to nature, then for Kauffman, nature is freighted with religious significance. Released from the "Galilean spell" of rigorous causal determinism, "We are well into a new scientific worldview in which we are members of a universe of creativity and history, a stunningly creative biosphere in which we cocreate" (141). It is in this awesome, continuous creativity that Kauffman discerns and proclaims as a new vision of religion. "The creativity in nature is God enough," he proclaims. "From this natural sense of God, we can hope to reinvent the sacred as the creativity in nature—without requiring that all that happens is to our liking. From that new sacred, we can hope to invent a global ethic to reorient our lives, and our emerging global civilization" (142).

I am greatly impressed by Kauffman's version of religious naturalism. He has worked throughout his book now under discussion to develop in careful detail a scientific interpretation of nature that gives prominence to its emergent processes and their truly remarkable creative outcomes. He is entirely right, in my judgment, in claiming that such a conception of nature readily invites a profound and lasting religious response.

But I have to disagree with his wanting to call the boundless creativity of nature *God*. I grant that he has in mind a thoroughly naturalistic meaning of this term, but its connotations, particularly in the Near East and the West, are bound to create confusion. This is so because God is commonly believed to be supernatural rather than natural and to have created nature instead of being a part of it. It is true that God is traditionally thought of as somehow immanent in nature, but God is also traditionally viewed as radically transcendent over nature and as preexisting nature. Moreover, God is typically conceived as a distinct personal being rather than as an aspect of an impersonal nature.

Kauffman is convinced that identifying God with the creativity of nature can help to inspire a global ethic and a new global religious attitude toward the earth and toward new ways of our behaving on it as human beings (273–80). It can give to religious faith a new sense of universality and common purpose among all of the peoples of the earth, with their diverse, presently existing religious traditions and communities of faith. Most importantly, it can focus primary attention on the well-being of the earth in a time of grave ecological danger.

But there is one fundamental problem with this way of "reinventing the sacred" in our time. That problem is simply that not all of the dominant religious traditions of nature are monotheistic or even theistic. *God* is not for all of them a religiously neutral word simply substitutable for them for their own particular focuses of ultimate religious faith and concern. It is in fact a provincial word, restricted to some religious traditions and not applicable for all. Far better, in my judgment, is the term *sacred*, which Kauffman also frequently uses. It is not God, whether immanent in nature or transcendent over it, or both, that gives promise of being the kind of reinvention that Kauffman dreams of and advocates. Rather, it is nature and the sacredness present everywhere in nature that qualifies for me, Raymo, and other religious naturalists as the appropriate focus of religious faith in a rapidly changing world.

Far more fitting and much less misleading is Kauffman's other term *sacred*, also contained in my last quotation of him above. In traditional theism, the sacredness of nature is derived from the sacredness of God. In religious naturalism it is primordial and underived. Nothing important would be lost, in my judgment, by getting rid of Kauffman's term *God* and replacing it with the term *sacred*. Its loss would be a significant gain in clarity and would also put him even more decisively in the camp of other religious naturalists. He belongs there as a highly regarded theoretical biologist and persuasive scientific developer and advocate for this religious outlook.

The Religious Naturalism of Philosopher Carol Wayne White

The last proponent of religious naturalism I want to feature here, in contrast with advocates for traditional monotheistic religions, commitments, and points of view, is that of religious philosopher Carol Wayne White. There are of course many other religious naturalists or commentators on religious naturalism who could have been used in this manner, including other female thinkers such as Connie Barlow, Ursula Goodenough, Stephanie Kaza, Jea Sophia Oh, Lisa H. Sideris, and Mary Evelyn Tucker. I provide a forum here for White's thought to round out my discussions of philosophers and other kinds of theorists discussed in this volume. Her perspective is an important complement to the other kinds of religious naturalism discussed so far in the last two chapters, including my own version of it and those of physicist Chet Raymo and biologist Stuart Kauffman. White entitles and subtitles the book that will be under discussion here, *Black Lives and Sacred Humanity: Toward an African American Spirituality*. In doing so, she adds the cultural dimension of pervasive racial discriminatory attitudes and segregation practices toward Black people in the United States to what she regards as religious naturalism's relevance as a commendable alternative to the traditional monotheistic religions of Judaism, Christianity, and Islam.

White and the three other Black writers on whose thought she draws and identifies as implicit religious naturalists akin in thought, spirit, and aspiration to herself, bring into glaring light the deplorable bad faith of much of traditional monotheism's preachments and practices with respect to Black people in the United States, from its inception to the present. The faith stance she envisions and defends is not one of alleged divine revelation and indisputable authority but one grounded in the probabilistic resources of human experience and reason. It is a religious faith that is deeply suspicious and dismissive of institutionally sanctioned absolutes and unquestioning appeals to what are too often regarded as literal, timeless absolutes of scriptural authority.

Her focus throughout is on nature rather than God, and most particularly on what she reverences as sacred humanity and its crucial role and responsibility within the natural order on earth. Her contention is that there is no need for appeal to an imagined supernatural authority or to voices from another world. All that we need is in this world, with its millions of nonhuman creatures and with one another as human creatures of this world—all deserving of high levels of respectful treatment and regard. Jesus's two great commandments are for White implicitly reducible to the second one of love for one's human neighbors because in learning how to reverence and love all other humans as sacred creatures of an inexhaustibly sacred nature we must also learn to love and carefully attend to the whole of nature and its other earthly creatures in whose ecological community humans are inseparable participants. Here are our destiny, privilege, and duty, and they lie within the whole span of our earthly lives. Here is all that we need spiritually as well as with regard to the more distinctively physical aspects of our nature. The earth is our natural and only home, and we share the mortality of its other living creatures.

White's whole orientation, like that of other religious naturalists, is toward this world, toward faithfulness to the needs of this world, and toward acceptance of our grave responsibilities to one another and to the nonhuman life forms and other aspects of this world. Sacredness and wonder lie all around us and place their awesome requirements on us here and now, not in some alleged purely spiritual, immaterial, everlasting realm to come. White's principal concern in her book is attitudes toward and treatments of Black humans like herself, but this concern is located squarely within the larger context of all humanity and an all-surrounding nature. She writes in one place that "humans are all genetically connected and part of a greater whole; any harm done to another human is essentially harm done to ourselves. No less important is appreciating how the concept of sacred humanity operates within religious naturalism to emphasize myriad layers of entanglement and essential connectivity—with oneself, one's family, the larger human community, myriad local and global ecosystems, and, yes, the universe" (2016, 35). Implicit in this emphasis on the multiple, inescapable aspects of human connectivity is the religious promotion of "kindness, empathy, and compassion for all natural processes, including human ones" (Ibid.).

Also implicit in this theme of *connectivity* throughout White's book is the closely related one of *liberation*, and especially the long striving of Black humans for freedom from the oppressive, unloving, condescending, and often contemptuous treatment of them—singly, collectively, and institutionally—by white people. The three Black authors she cites in these respects are especially notable, in her view, and rightfully so, for their palpable, persistent, and eloquent pleas to be recognized and treated as human beings in a thoroughly loving and grateful manner.

The three of them—Anna Julia Cooper, W. E. B. Du Bois, and James Baldwin—are accorded central roles in her book of giving poignant expression to this liberationist theme in the face of widespread, persistent historical failures of whites to acknowledge and treat Black people equally as fellow humans. In doing so, the three writers implicitly give expression to the urgent need for some kind of truly transformative religious outlook and truly effective, all-inclusive recognition of the inviolable sacredness of *all* humankind.

We should note that the civil rights movement of the middle of the past century shows that Black people did not just wait in yearning, prayerful near-despair to be treated with dignity by whites. Writers like Cooper, Du Bois, and Baldwin helped to motivate and inspire this movement by giving powerful, poignant, eloquent literary expression to Black people's desperate yearnings for their liberation. Later Black leaders like Martin Luther King Jr. were able to organize and fight for effective responses to such yearnings by various kinds of public protest, sit-ins, boycotts, marches, and political pressures.

Especially notable in this respect were King's meetings concerning racial justice with Presidents John F. Kennedy and Lyndon Baines Johnson. In consequence of these meetings, against the background of the organized actions of Black people as a whole, federal laws were passed, Black voting was legally protected, schools, restaurants, stores, movie theaters, and other establishments were integrated, and segregation barriers were torn down. This was progress, but important areas of toleration and inclusion still await much-needed further changes, and especially those of deep-rooted prejudicial attitudes and failures of acceptance by whites of the dignity, rights, and full humanity of Black people everywhere in the United States.

For White, failure to recognize and honor liberation's central importance in Black religious and secular history would be a shamefully deplorable, deeply regrettable, notably glaring defect in any religious perspective. But it is especially inconsistent, and radically so, with regard to religious naturalism as a viable, lastingly important religious outlook. Nature is replete with interconnections and entanglements of many different kinds—human and otherwise. And as White argues, these cry out everywhere for recognition and respect, expressed in social attitudes and equitably administered laws. It is also essential for her that they become deeply rooted in *religious* outlooks and practices

White's humanism and her reverence for nature are inseparably conjoined in her conception of religious naturalism. As I am sure she would readily agree, the whole of nature on this earth is in desperate need of *liberation* from the rampant neglects, misuses, and oppressions that continue to be inflicted on its human and nonhuman creatures and their places in an all-surrounding, radically diverse, but also profusely interconnected nature by willfully insensitive, unempathetic, uncaring human beings. She makes a crucial and distinctive contribution by closely connecting religious naturalism with forceful emphasis on *sacred humanity* as an essential aspect of sacred nature here on earth, and on the liberating reverence, commitment, wonder, and love evoked and demanded by authentic religious faith.

Conclusion

We have traveled a considerable distance in this book. I have presented and criticized arguments on behalf of monotheism's traditional conception of God. These arguments range from appeals to divine revelation to those based on reason, natural science, and religious experience. None of them stands up successfully, in my view, to critical scrutiny, and I have tried to show why I believe this to be the case. A chapter on Ludwig Feuerbach's argument to the effect that that the theistic God is an unconscious imaginative projection of humans onto the universe (or, more accurately, pluriverse) as a whole and as its ultimate source and explanation helped to make this case.

Instead of trying to explain the existence of nature and central features of nature by means of their creation by an omni-attributed, personal God, I introduced in the final two chapters a concept of the sacred associated *solely* with nature. I showed how I personally envision and defend this conception and complemented my defense with those of three highly esteemed fellow-religious naturalists, Chet Raymo, Stuart A. Kauffman, and Carol Wayne White, the first one a physicist, the second, a theoretical biologist, and the third, a philosopher. In this manner, I have sought to bring into perspective a credible alternative to traditional theism, and one consistent with congenial forms of scientific naturalism.

In an entry entitled "Religious Naturalism" contained in *The Routledge Companion to Philosophy of Religion*, edited by Chad Meister and Paul Copan and published in 2007, I presented seven "merits" of religious naturalism (680). I reiterate versions of them here as a fitting conclusion to the present book. I hope that they will help to explicate and explain why religious naturalism means so much to me and to make clear its strong appeal to others of similar conviction.

First, there is in religious naturalism no in-principle conflict with scientific attempts to understand, interpret, and explain aspects of the natural world. The natural sciences bring into view countless sacred wonders of nature that would otherwise be unrecognized and unknown. Second, there is no need for appeal to a dubious supernatural world believed by many to lie beyond this world. There is more than enough in this world to awaken and nurture our religious sensibilities and yearnings. Third, religious naturalism invites us to come to terms with our finitude as natural beings rather than desperately trying to overcome it. This is admittedly no easy task, but religious naturalism can be equal to it when its character and resources are properly discerned.

Fourth, religious naturalism is not preoccupied with personal salvation beyond the grave, but is freed from that preoccupation to enable us to attend conscientiously to life on earth and to the many urgent needs of living beings on earth—including, but not restricted to, those of our own species. Fifth, it enables us to give thanks for the earth as our natural home and for our existence as creatures of nature made in its image rather than in the image of an imagined supernatural God. Instead of trying to convince us that we are something we are not, it encourages us to strive and live as the extraordinary material creatures we are.

Sixth, it enables us to feel an integral part of the community of living creatures on earth rather than viewing humans as apart from them and entitled to dominate them and use them in any way we see fit—a recipe for imminent global disaster. Seventh, religious naturalism encourages us to think for ourselves and to rely on our own intelligence and agential capabilities as gifts of nature rather than having need for saving visions and resources from some other world. We can give to sacred, immanent, wondrous nature the reverence and commitment formerly reserved for a distant, inscrutable God ironically fashioned in the image of a human being. These merits of religious naturalism deserve careful consideration and should not be dismissed or overlooked by those of a theistic persuasion.

Notes

Introduction

1. The idea of *secular* forms of faith may sound strange to those used to viewing faith as being an exclusively religious phenomenon. But I use the term *faith* in a much more general sense as its being applicable to those forms of confidence, trust, and commitment that can characterize secular as well as religious persons and traditions—forms that impart to their lives overarching, crucial, and pervasive aspects of existential meaning, importance, and value. Wholehearted commitment to Marxism as a way of life might function as a secular form of faith, for example. Secular forms of faith can therefore subserve important *functions* similar to those of familiar forms of religious faith, while not sharing religions' distinctive kinds of *ontological commitment* (see Crosby 2018a: 74–78 and 2022: 122–26). I owe the important distinction between commonalities of *function*, on the one hand, and differences of *ontological belief*, on the other, to philosopher Kevin Schilbrack. See his 2013 article listed in the bibliography of the present book.

Chapter Four

1. See Crosby 2020, chapters 4 and 5. I should add here that I also regard space as derivative from the quantum realm, and therefore not as primordial, in the way that matter-energy and time are.

Chapter Five

1. See in this connection Crosby 2013. Nature has innumerable "thous" that deserve religious respect and conscientious moral treatment. These include

not just humans but all sentient creatures, especially those with relatively high levels of conscious awareness. They are not things but living beings like ourselves and can and should be appreciated and related to as such.

Chapter Seven

1. I allude here to the appropriate title of the perceptive book by Loyal Rue: *Nature is Enough: Religious Naturalism and the Meaning of Life.*

2. For more extensive discussion of the question of whether the ambiguities of nature disqualify it as an appropriate focus of religious commitment, see Crosby 2008 and 2010.

Chapter Eight

1. For a discussion of Raymo's religious naturalism and comparison of it with the views of the thoughtful contemporary Christian theist Diana Butler Bass (2017) see chapter 8 of Crosby 2022. Bass's emphasis is on a radically immanent God rather than a radically transcendent God—in other words, a God grounded in nature rather than being outside of it. So the comparison with Raymo is an especially interesting one.

Bass's conception of God, however, is never made clear in her book, as I point out in mine. Is a radically immanent "God" any different, in the final analysis, than a profound sense of the sacredness of nature itself such as that so beautifully and compellingly recounted in Raymo's book? I raise a similar question about Stuart Kauffman's book to be described and analyzed in the next section, where Kauffman identifies the creativity of nature with God.

Bibliography

Allan, George. 2020. *Whitehead's Radically Temporalist Metaphysics: Recovering the Seriousness of Time*. Lanham, MD: Lexington Books.

Bass, Diana Butler. 2017. *Grounded: Finding God in the World; A Spiritual Revolution*. New York: Harper One.

Bible, The Holy. 1962. Revised Standard Version, Oxford Annotated, ed. Herbert G. May and Bruce M. Metzger. New York: Oxford University Press.

Buber, Martin. 1970. *I and Thou*, ed., trans. Walter Kaufmann. New York: Simon and Schuster.

Christian, William A. 1964. *Meaning and Truth in Religion*. Princeton, NJ: Princeton University Press.

Corrington, Robert S. 2013. *Nature's Sublime: An Essay in Aesthetic Naturalism*. Lanham, MD: Lexington Books.

Crosby, Donald A. 2002. *A Religion of Nature*. Albany: State University of New York Press.

———. 2008. *Living with Ambiguity: Religious Naturalism and the Menace of Evil*. Albany: State University of New York Press.

———. 2010. "Both Red and Green but Religiously Right: Coping with Evil in a Religion of Nature." *American Journal of Theology and Philosophy*, 31/2, May.

———. 2011. *Faith and Reason: Their Roles in Religious and Secular Life*. Albany: State University of New York Press.

———. 2013. *The Thou of Nature: Religious Naturalism and Reverence for Sentient Life*. Albany: State University of New York Press.

———. 2015. *Nature as Sacred Ground: A Metaphysics for Religious Naturalism*. Albany: State University of New York Press.

———. 2018a. *Faith and Freedom: Contexts, Choices, and Crises in Religious Commitments*. New York: Routledge.

———. 2018b. "The Abrahamic Faiths as Forces for Good or Evil." *American Journal of Theology and Philosophy*, 39/3, September, 29–47.

———. 2020. *Primordial Time: Its Irreducible Reality, Human Significance, and Ecological Importance.* Lanham, MD: Lexington Books.

———. 2022. *Sacred and Secular: Responses to Life in a Finite World.* Albany: State University of New York Press.

———. 2023. *Evolutionary Emergence of Purposive Goals and Values: A Naturalistic Teleology.* Albany: State University of New York Press.

Dawkins, Richard. 1987. *The Blind Watchmaker: Why the Evidence of Evolution Reveals a Universe Without Design.* New York: W. W. Norton.

Dewey, John. 1934. *A Common Faith.* New Haven, CT: Yale University Press.

Feuerbach, Ludwig. 2008. *The Essence of Christianity*, trans. George Eliot. Mineola, NY: Dover Publications.

Goodenough, Ursula. 2023. *The Sacred Depths of Nature: How Life has Emerged and Evolved.* 2nd ed. New York: Oxford University Press.

Hume, David. 1957. *Dialogues Concerning Natural Religion*, ed. Henry D. Aiken. New York

Heidegger, Martin. 1996. *Being and Time: A Translation of Sein und Zeit*, trans. Joan Stambaugh. Albany: State University of New York Press.

Hogue, Michael S. 2010. *The Promise of Religious Naturalism.* Lanham, MD: Rowman & Littlefield.

Husserl, Edmund. 2019. *The Phenomenology of Internal Time Consciousness*, ed. Martin Heidegger, trans. James S. Churchill. Bloomington: Indiana University Press.

James, William. 1929. *The Varieties of Religious Experience.* New York: The Modern Library.

Kauffman, Stuart A. 2008. *Reinventing the Sacred: A New View of Science, Reason and Religion.* New York: Basic Books.

Kierkegaard, Søren. 1936. *Philosophical Fragments or A Fragment of Philosophy*, trans. David F. Swenson. Princeton, NJ: Princeton University Press.

———. 1941. *Fear and Trembling*, trans. Walter Lowrie. Princeton, NJ: Princeton University Press

———. 1944. *Kierkegaard's Concluding Unscientific Postscript*, trans. David F. Swenson and Walter Lowrie. Princeton, NJ: Princeton University Press.

———. 1951. *The Sickness Unto Death*, trans. Walter Lowrie. Princeton, NJ: Princeton University Press.

Meister, Chad, and Paul Copan, eds. 2007. *The Routledge Companion to Philosophy of Religion.* New York: Routledge.

Nabokov, Valdimir. September 4, 2023. "Butterflies: The Childhood of a Lepidopterist." *The New Yorker*, 16–19. Reprinted from "Reflections," in *The New Yorker* of June 12, 1948.

Polkinghorne, John. 1998. *Belief in God in an Age of Science*. New Haven, CT: Yale University Press.

———. 2002. *Faith, Science and Understanding*. New Haven, CT: Yale University Press.

Raymo, Chet. 1987. *Honey from Stone: A Naturalist's Search for God*. Cambridge, MA: Cowley Publications.

———. 1999. *Natural Prayers*. Saint Paul, MN: Ruminator Books.

———. 2008. *When God is Gone Everything is Holy: The Making of a Religious Naturalist*. Notre Dame, IN: Sorin Books.

Rue, Loyal. 2011. *Nature is Enough: Religious Naturalism and the Meaning of Life*. Albany: State University of New York Press.

Sartre, Jean-Paul. 1948. *Existentialism and Humanism*, trans. Philip Mairet. Brooklyn, NY: Haskell House Publishers.

Schelling, F. W. J. 2020. *Philosophy of Revelation (1841–42), and Related Texts*, ed. Klaus Ottmann. Thompson, CT: Spring Publications.

Schilbrack, Kevin. 2013. "What Isn't Religion?" *Journal of Religion* 93, no. 3 (July): 291–319.

Stone, Jerome A. 2008. *Religious Naturalism Today: The Rebirth of a Forgotten Alternative*. Albany: State University of New York Press.

Swinburne, Richard. 2004. *The Existence of God: Second Edition*. Oxford: Clarendon Press.

Tennant, F. R. 1930. *Philosophical Theology, Vol. II: The World, the Soul, and God*. Cambridge: Cambridge University Press.

Tillich, Paul. 1948. *The Shaking of the Foundations*. New York: Charles Scribner's Sons.

———. 1951. *Systematic Theology*, Volume I. Chicago: University of Chicago Press.

———. 1952. *The Courage to Be*. New Haven, CT: Yale University Press.

———. 1957. *Dynamics of Faith*. New York: Harper Torchbooks.

White, Carol Wayne. 2016. *Black Lives and Sacred Humanity: Toward An African American Religious Naturalism*. New York: Fordham University Press.

Whitehead, Alfred North. 1975. *Process and Reality: Corrected Edition*, edited by David Ray Griffin and Donald W. Sherburne. New York: The Free Press.

Index

Systematic Theology (Tillich), 46

technical devices, for awareness,
123–124
temptation, of Jesus of Nazareth, 15,
72
Tennant, F. R., 102
Terry Lectures, 90
Tertullian (Father), 43
"thatness" (*quod*), 65, 66
theism, 99–100
ontology relation to, 54
science relation to, 82
theocratic state, authority in, 33
theologians, 87, 88
theological metaphysics, 82, 84, 88,
146
revelation relation to, 83, 86–87
"theory of everything" and, 89–90
theology, 9
natural, 74, 88
natural science relation to, 84
religion compared to, 95–96
science relation to, 92
self-disclosure relation to, 87–88
"theory of everything," 84, 89–90
thought, 14, 30, 37, 56, 81–82
Tillich, Paul, 4–6, 8–9, 44, 48–49, 86
on Being-Itself, 52–53, 55–56,
61, 66, 78, 86
on courage, 51, 52, 98
The Courage to Be of, 45
Feuerbach compared to, 64
on finitude, 46, 47, 58, 60, 131
on nature, 57, 97
Polkinghorne compared to, 84–85
Schelling relation to, 63, 69
on symbols, 54–55, 59, 71–72

time, 123
matter-energy and, 108, 157n1
(Chapter Four)
mind relation to, 102
omniscience relation to, 37
paradox and, 18
primordial nature of, 77
tradition, 50, 54, 69
transformation, 50, 67
creation as, 107–108, 123
newness relation to, 76–77
revelation relation to, 16, 17–18,
19, 34, 40–41
from sin, 38
trials, of human beings, 107
Trinitarian Christianity, 34, 40
trinitarianism, 71
Triune God, 4, 38, 39, 40, 71
truth, 8, 23, 26, 29, 90

uncertainty, 127
understanding, 7, 41, 74, 123–124
in finitude, 78
mutual, 120–121
revelation relation to, 20
uniformity, 120
United States
Black people in, 150–153
White Christian Nationalism in,
3
urgrund ("nameless abyss"), 63–64

The Varieties of Religious Experience
(James), 121
violence, religion relation to, 119

Wallace, Alfred Russel, 68, 91
well-being, 129, 132